The Cumberland Presbyterian Handbook

About the "Log Cabin"

Having some fun and depicting the Log Cabin indicates that even though theology is serious stuff, we should nonetheless remember that it is not our theology that saves us, but Jesus Christ. Therefore, our life in the church can be buoyant, and our theological wranglings can be done with a sense of humor and love for our neighbor.

The Cumberland Presbyterian Handbook

The Ministry Council
of the General Assembly
of the Cumberland Presbyterian Church
Cordova, Tennessee

© 2012 Ministry Council of the General Assembly of the Cumberland Presbyterian Church.

Presbyterian-specific components adapted from The Presbyterian Handbook originally published by Geneva Press © 2006.

Part of this book was originally published as *The Lutheran Handbook* © 2005 Augsburg Fortress.

All rights reserved. No part of this book may be reproduced or transmitted in any form or by any means, electronic or mechanical, including photocopying, recording, or by any information storage or retrieval system, without permission in writing from the publisher. For information, address Geneva Press, 100 Witherspoon Street, Louisville, Kentucky 40202-1396.

Scripture quotations from the New Revised Standard Version of the Bible are copyright © 1989 by the Division of Christian Education of the National Council of the Churches of Christ in the U.S.A. and are used by permission.

Pages 65–78: Sources for the charts include reference materials from *Information Please*, ® New York Times Public Library/Hyperion, Rose Publishing, Time-Life, and Wadsworth Group/Thomas Learning.

Book design by James Satter
Interior illustrations: Brenda Brown and Fernando Ruiz
Cover design by Dean Nicklas
Cover illustration: Jaime Groce

Contributing writers: Julie Bowe, Mark Brown, Suzanne Burke, Lou Carlozo, Giacomo Cassese, Mark Gardner, Wes Halula, Sara Henrich, Mark Hinton, Sue Houglum, Rolf Jacobson, Susan M. Lang, Andrea Lee, Daniel Levitin, Terry Marks, Catherine Malotky, Donald K. McKim, Jeffrey S. Nelson, Rebecca Ninke, Eliseo Pérez-Álvarez, Dawn Rundman, Jonathan Rundman, Ted Schroeder, Ken Sundet-Jones, Hans Wiersma

Elements of *Worst-Case Scenario Survival Handbook* trade dress have been used with permission of and under license from Quirk Productions, Inc. Based on the trade dress of *The Worst-Case Scenario Survival Handbook* Series, by Joshua Piven and David Borgenicht, published by Chronicle Books, LLC, *Worst-Case Scenario and The Worst-Case Scenario Survival Handbook* are registered trademarks of Quirk Productions, Inc., 215 Church Street, Philadelphis, PA 19106.

ISBN: 978-0-615-29363-9

PRINTED IN THE UNITED STATES OF AMERICA

CONTENTS

This Book Belongs To	10
About My Congregation	11
Preface	12

Church Stuff   15

How to Get to Know Your Pastor	16
How to Survive for One Hour in an Unair-conditioned Church	18
How to Respond When Someone Sits in Your Pew	20
How to Use a Worship Bulletin	21
How to Sing a Hymn	24
How to Sing a Praise Song	26
How to Listen to a Sermon	28
How to Respond to a Disruption during Worship	31
Sacraments	34
The Anatomy of a Baptism	35
Infant and Younger Children	35
Adult and Older Children	36
How to Receive the Lord's Supper	37
Six Questions and Answers about the Lord's Supper	39
How to Pass the Plate	42
How to Share the Peace in Church	45
How to Stay Alert in Church	47

What to Bring to a Church Potluck (by Region)	49
Cumberland Presbyterian Origins	53
The Presbyterian Family in the United States	55
Big-Time Ancestors & Leaders for Cumberland Presbyterians	56
Five Facts about Life in Medieval Times	58
History's Six Most Notorious Heretics	60
How to Avoid Getting Burned at the Stake	62

Charts and Diagrams

World Religions	65
Comparative Religions	66
Family Tree of Christianity	68
U.S. Christian Denominations	69
Comparative Denominations	70
The Seasons of the Church Year and What They Mean	74
The Seasons of the Church Year (diagram)	76
Cumberland Presbyterian Symbol	78

Everyday Stuff 79

How to Understand the Relationship between the Law and Grace	80
How to Know What God Wants You to Do with Your Life	83
How Cumberland Presbyterians Understand Evangelism	84
How to Pray	85
How to Work for Peace and Justice on Behalf of People Who Are Poor and Oppressed	87

How to Identify a Genuine Miracle	89
Three Essential Personal Spiritual Practices	91
How to Forgive Someone	94
How to Care for the Sick	96
How to Identify and Deal with Evil	98
How to Avoid Gossip	100
How to Resolve Interpersonal Conflict	102
How to Console Someone	104
How to Cope with Loss and Grief	105
The Top Ten Attributes to Look for in a Spouse	107
How to Be Saved (by Grace through Faith and Not by Your Good Works)	110
How to Understand the Trinity as One God in Three Persons	113
How to Talk to Friends About the Cumberland Presbyterian Church	116

Bible Stuff   121

Common Translations of the Bible	122
60 Essential Bible Stories	124
How to Read the Bible	127
How to Interpret the Bible	129
How to Memorize a Bible Verse	131
Ten Bible Villains	134
Ten Bible Heroes	137
The Three Most Rebellious Things Jesus Did	140
The Seven Funniest Bible Stories	141

The Five Grossest Bible Stories	144
Five Facts about Life in Old Testament Times	146
Ten Important Things That Happened between the Old and New Testaments	147
Five Facts about Life in New Testament Times	150
The Five Biggest Misconceptions about the Bible	152
Jesus' Twelve Apostles (Plus Judas and Paul)	154
The Five Weirdest Laws in the Old Testament	157
The Top Ten Bible Miracles and What They Mean	159

Maps and Diagrams

The Exodus	161
The Holy Land—Old Testament Times	162
The Holy Land—New Testament Times	163
Paul's Journeys	164
Jerusalem in Jesus' Time	166
Noah's Ark	167
The Ark of the Covenant	168
Solomon's Temple	169
The Armor of God	170
The Crucifixion	171

Cumberland Presbyterian Stuff 175

The Church on a Mission from God	176
The Church Reformed and Always Being Reformed	177
Key Cumberland Presbyterian Concepts	178
Church Government	180

Cumberland Presbyterian Lingo	181
Ordination and Installation	182

Confessing the Faith   183

Creeds and Confessions	184
The *Confession of Faith*	185
Key Comments from the Confession	186
Tips on Interpreting the *Confession of Faith*	189
Two Creeds	191
The Nicene Creed	192
The Apostles' Creed	194
Cumberland Presbyterian Catechism	195
The Catechism: Selected Q&A	196
Open to the Spirit	199

For Further Study   201

Books for Cumberland Presbyterians to Read	202

Notes and stuff   204

This Book Belongs To

Name _____

Address _____

_____

E-mail _____

Telephone _____

Birth date _____

Baptismal birth date _____

First communion _____

Confirmation date _____

Godparents' (baptismal sponsors') names

_____

_____

_____

_____

Churches I've belonged to	Years of membership
_____	_____
_____	_____
_____	_____
_____	_____
_____	_____
_____	_____

About My Congregation

Name _____

Address _____
_____

Year organized/founded _____

My pastor(s) _____
_____
_____
_____

Number of baptized members _____

Average weekly worship attendance _____

Facts about my denomination _____
_____
_____
_____

Other information about my congregation and faith
_____
_____
_____
_____

PREFACE

Please Be Advised:

Lots of books, pamphlets, and booklets have been written through the centuries as companions for average folks who wanted help navigating their way through a complicated subject. *The Boy Scout Handbook* comes to mind, for example. So do *The American Red Cross First Aid and Safety Handbook, Tune and Repair Your Own Piano: A Practical and Theoretical Guide to the Tuning of All Keyboard Stringed Instruments,* and *National Audubon Society's Field Guide to North American Reptiles and Amphibians.* They stand as testimony to the average person's need for a guide to both the vast truths and complex detail that make up a particular area of interest. These books turn complicated, inaccessible ideas into simple, easy-to-understand concepts, and, if necessary, into action steps that are easy to follow.

Likewise, THE CUMBERLAND PRESBYTERIAN HANDBOOK follows this format. Here, you will discover a combination of reliable, historical, and theological information alongside some fun facts and very practical tips on being a churchgoing follower of Jesus Christ, all presented in that oh-so-Cumberland Presbyterian, down-to-earth, tongue-in-cheek sort of way.

You will also discover that this book is intended for learning and enjoyment. (Some Cumberland Presbyterians have trouble doing the latter until they've first suffered through the former.) It's meant to spur conversation, to inform and edify, and to make you laugh. Think of the book as a comedian with a dry sense of humor and a degree in theology. It can be used in the classroom with students or at the dinner table with family or in solitude.

But however you use it, use it! We've cut the corners off so you can throw it in your backpack or stuff it in a pocket. It's printed on paper that accepts either ink or pencil nicely, so feel free to write and highlight in it (and there's room for notes in the back). The cover is this fancy, nearly indestructible stuff that will last forever too, so don't worry about spilling soda pop or coffee on it. We've even heard it can sustain a direct hit from a nuclear missile.

Anyway, the point is this: Being a follower of Jesus is hard enough without having to navigate the faith journey—let alone the maze of church culture—all alone. Sooner or later everyone needs a companion.

—The Editors

CHURCH STUFF

Every well-prepared Cumberland Presbyterian should have a basic understanding of church teachings and where they came from.

Plus, since every congregation goes about worship in a slightly different way, it might take a little time to get the hang of things—especially if you're new to a congregation.

This section includes:

- Essential facts about the Cumberland Presbyterian faith. (If you know these things, you'll know more than most.)
- Practical advice for singing hymns, taking Communion, and getting to know the people in your congregation.
- Hints for enjoying worship—even when you're having a bad day.

HOW TO GET TO KNOW YOUR PASTOR

Pastors play an important role in the daily life of your congregation and the community. Despite their churchly profession, fancy robes, and knowledge of theology, pastors experience the same kinds of ups and downs as everyone else. They value member efforts to meet, connect with, and support them.

❶ Connect with your pastor after worship.
After the worship service, join others in line to shake the pastor's hand. Sharing a comment about the sermon, readings, or hymns lets the pastor know that his or her worship planning time is appreciated. If your congregation doesn't practice the dismissal line, find other ways to make that personal connection.

❷ Pray daily for your pastor, because he or she doesn't just work on Sunday.
Your pastor has many responsibilities, like visiting members in the hospital, writing sermons, and figuring out who can help drain the flooded church basement. In your prayers, ask God to grant your pastor health, strength, and wisdom to face the many challenges of leading a congregation.

❸ Ask your pastor to share with you why he or she entered ordained ministry.
There are many reasons why a pastor may have enrolled in seminary to become an ordained minister. Be prepared for a story that may surprise you.

❹ Stop by your pastor's office to talk, or consider making an appointment to get to know him or her. Pastors welcome the opportunity to connect with church members at times other than worship. As you would with any drop-in visit, be sensitive to the fact that your pastor may be quite busy. A scheduled appointment just to chat could provide a welcome break in your pastor's day.

Getting to know your pastor can help you to get more out of church.

HOW TO SURVIVE FOR ONE HOUR IN AN UNAIR-CONDITIONED CHURCH

Getting trapped in an overheated sanctuary is a common churchgoing experience. The key is to minimize your heat gain and electrolyte loss.

❶ Plan ahead.
When possible, scout out the sanctuary ahead of time to locate optimal seating near fans or open windows. Consider where the sun will be during the worship service and avoid sitting under direct sunlight. Bring a bottle of water for each person in your group.

❷ Maintain your distance from others.
Human beings disperse heat and moisture as a means of cooling themselves. An average-size person puts off about as much heat as a 75-watt lightbulb. The front row will likely be empty and available.

❸ Remain still.
Fidgeting will only make your heat index rise.

Use your bulletin as a personal fan to keep cool.

④ During Communion, if wine and grape juice are offered, choose grape juice. Alcohol is a dehydrator (diuretic), and dehydration is bad. The miniscule amount of alcohol in Communion wine is unlikely to cause dehydration, but err on the side of caution

⑤ Dress for survival.
Wear only cool, breathable fabrics.

⑥ Avoid acolyte or choir robes when possible.
Formal robes are especially uncomfortable in the heat. If you must wear one, make sure to wear lightweight clothes underneath.

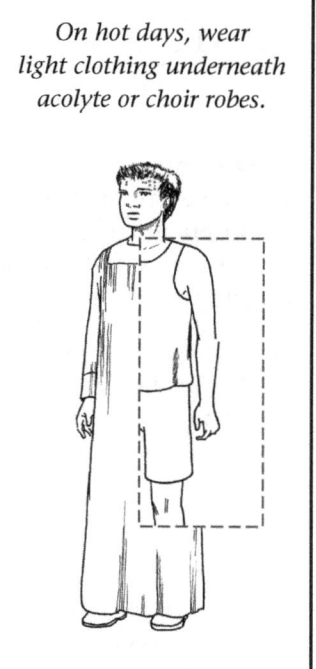

On hot days, wear light clothing underneath acolyte or choir robes.

⑦ Pray.
Jesus survived on prayer in the desert for 40 days. Lifting and extending your arms in an open prayer position may help cool your body by dispersing excess heat. If you've been perspiring, though, avoid exposing others to your personal odor.

Be Aware
- Carry a personal fan—or use your bulletin as a substitute.
- Worship services scheduled for one hour sometimes will run long. Plan ahead.

HOW TO RESPOND WHEN SOMEONE SITS IN YOUR PEW

We all carry a bubble of personal space. For some people, it's several feet. For others, it's about a half an inch. Wherever on the spectrum you fall, there are certain situations in which we invite visitors into our sphere of experience—like at church. Furthermore, human beings are territorial in nature and sometimes see strangers inside the bubble as an affront. These situations need not be cause for alarm.

❶ Smile and greet the "intruders."
Oftentimes they are visitors to your congregation—new blood. Avoid creating bad blood you might regret later on. Make solid eye contact so they know you mean it, shake hands with them, and leave no impression that they've done something wrong.

❷ View the "intrusion" as an opportunity.
Remember, you don't own the pew; you just borrow it once a week. Take the opportunity to get out of your rut and sit someplace new. This will physically emphasize a change in your perspective and may yield new spiritual discoveries.

❸ If you can tell that your new friends feel uncomfortable at having displaced you, despite your efforts to the contrary, make an extra effort to welcome them.
Consider taking them to brunch after church to become acquainted. If there are too many for you to foot the bill, consider inviting them to accompany you on a "go Dutch" basis. This will eliminate any hierarchy and place you on equal footing.

HOW TO USE A WORSHIP BULLETIN

Many Cumberland Presbyterian congregations offer a printed resource called a bulletin to assist worshipers. The bulletin may contain the order of the service, liturgical information, music listings, the day's Bible readings, and important community announcements.

1. **Arrive early.**
   A few extra minutes before worship will allow you to scan the bulletin and prepare for the service.

2. **Receive the bulletin from the usher.**
   Upon entering the worship space, an usher will give you a bulletin. Some congregations stack bulletins near the entrance for self-service.

3. **Review the order of worship.**
   When seated, open the bulletin and find the order of the service, usually printed on the first or second page.

4. **Determine if other worship resources are required.**
   The order of worship may specify hymnals, song sheets, candles, or other external supplies required during the service.

5. **Fill out the attendance card.**
   A card may be located inside the bulletin or somewhere in your row. Fill it out completely. Resist the temptation to devise a clever "alias." The church office staff will not be amused. You may be asked to pass this card to an usher or to place it in the offering plate. Some congregations have attendance books for people to sign.

6 Reflect on bulletin artwork.
Covers often feature a drawing or design that corresponds to the season of the church year or the day's Bible verses. Examine the artwork and make a note of its connection to the lessons or sermon.

7 Track your worship progress.
The bulletin will guide you through the liturgy, hymns, and lessons as you worship and let you know where you are at all times.

8 Watch for liturgical dialogues.
The bulletin may contain spoken parts of the liturgy not found in the hymnal. The worship leader's parts may be marked with a "P:" or "L:". The congregation's responses may be marked with a "C:" or "All:" and are often printed in boldface type.

9 Identify the worship leaders and assistants.
The names of ushers, musicians, greeters, readers, acolytes, and pastors usually can be found in the bulletin. Greet these people by name following the service.

10 Review the printed announcements.
Community activities, calendars, and updates are often listed on the back of the bulletin. Scan listings during the prelude music, the offering, or the spoken announcements.

11 Make good use of the bulletin after the service.
Some congregations re-use bulletins for later services. Return the bulletin if possible. Recycling bins may also be provided. If you wish, or unless otherwise instructed, you may take the bulletin home with you.

Be Aware

- Many church secretaries and worship committees need help preparing the bulletin each week. You may want to volunteer to copy, fold, or assemble the bulletin for an upcoming service.
- Bulletins provide instructions on when the congregation should stand and sit. Many times Cumberland Presbyterian Churches will use an asterisk (*) to indicate when it is appropriate to stand. The bulletin may note also that worshipers may stand "when able." This is to recognize the needs of those who are unable to stand. It also reminds us that true participation in worship does not depend on either standing or sitting. The goal is for all God's children to worship God in the midst of the congregation.

If you choose not to save your worship bulletin, be sure to recycle it whenever possible.

HOW TO SING A HYMN

Music is an important part of the Christian tradition and an enjoyable way to build community. Hymn singing can be done without demonstrable emotion, but many otherwise reserved Cumberland Presbyterians appropriately channel emotion into their hymn singing and are therefore loud.

❶ Locate hymns in advance.
Consult the worship bulletin or the hymn board to find numbers for the day's hymns. Bookmark these pages in the hymnal using an offering envelope or attendance card. If you are thinking of tearing the corners from your bulletin to use as place holders, don't bother. They are too small and slip down between the pages and become confetti for the next person who uses the hymnal.

❷ Familiarize yourself with the hymns.
Examine the composer credits, the years the composer(s) lived, and whether the tune has a name different from the hymn itself. Note how the hymn is categorized in the hymnal. Many hymnals group the songs into categories, such as "Opening Hymns" and "Christmas."

❸ Assist nearby visitors or children.
Using a hymnal can be confusing. If your neighbors seem disoriented, help them find the correct pages, or let them read from your book.

❹ Adopt a posture for best vocal performance.
Hold the hymnal away from your body at chest level. Place one hand under the spine of the binding, leaving the other hand free to turn the pages. Keep your chin up so your voice projects outward.

❺ Begin singing.
If the hymn is unfamiliar, sing the melody for the first verse. If you read music, explore the written harmony parts during the remaining verses. Loud-singing neighbors may or may not be in tune, follow them with caution.

Support the hymnal's spine with one hand. Place the other on the open page.

❻ Focus on the hymn's content.
Some of the lyrics may connect with a Scripture reading of the day. Certain ones may be especially inspiring.

❼ Avoid dreariness.
Hymns are often sung in such a serious way that the congregation forgets to enjoy the music. Sing with energy and feeling.

Be Aware

- Hymnals are not just for use at church. Consider keeping a personal copy of your congregation's hymnal at home for further reference and study. Hymnals also make excellent baptism or confirmation gifts.

- Some hymns use words and phrases that are difficult to understand (such as, "Here I raise my Ebenezer," from the hymn "Come, Thou Fount of Every Blessing"). Use a dictionary or a Bible with a concordance to clear up any uncertainty.

Church Stuff

HOW TO SING A PRAISE SONG

Many Cumberland Presbyterian congregations use modern worship styles, often called Praise & Worship (P&W), featuring guitars and drums. In these settings the words are typically displayed on large, multimedia projection screens.

❶ Follow the instructions of the song leader.
Someone in the praise band will invite the congregation to stand up, sit down, repeat certain sections, or divide into men's and women's vocal parts. Pay attention to this person to avoid getting off track.

❷ Learn the melody and song structure.
Pay special attention to the melody line sung by the band's lead vocalist. Praise & Worship songs can be tricky because they are rarely printed with notated sheet music and are sung differently from place to place.

❸ Sing along with gusto.
Once the melody has been introduced, join in the singing. When you're comfortable with the song, experiment with harmony parts.

❹ Avoid "zoning out."
Singing lyrics that are projected on giant screens can result in a glazed-over facial expression. Avoid this by surveying the worship area, noticing paraments and liturgical symbols, and making eye contact with other people.

❺ Identify lyrical themes.
Determine if the song is being used as a confession, a prayer, a hymn of praise, or serves another purpose.

⑥ Watch out for raised hands.
Some Cumberland Presbyterians emote while singing contemporary Christian songs and may suddenly raise their hands in praise to God. Give them plenty of room to avoid losing your eyeglasses. If you are moved to raise your hands in praise, go more vertical than horizontal.

Be Aware

- Worship in Cumberland Presbyterian Churches is highly participatory. The praise band is there to help you sing and participate in worship, not to perform a concert.
- There are no prohibitions in the Cumberland Presbyterian tradition against physical expression during worship. However, in some congregations, praise gestures will draw amused stares.

Beware of especially passionate worshipers who might raise their hands too quickly.

Church Stuff

HOW TO LISTEN TO A SERMON

Cumberland Presbyterians believe God's Word comes to us through the sacraments and the preaching of Holy Scripture. Honoring God's Word, not to mention getting something out of church, includes diligent listening to the sermon and active mental participation.

❶ Review active listening skills.
While the listener in this case doesn't get to speak, the sermon is still a conversation. Make mental notes as you listen. Take notice of where and why you react and which emotions you experience.

❷ Take notes.
Note-taking promotes active listening and provides a good basis for later reflection. It also allows you to return to confusing or complicated parts at your own leisure. Some congregations provide space in the bulletin for notes. If not, consider tucking a notepad in your purse or pocket.

Take notes to recall more information and get more out of the sermon.

Try taking notes in an outline form so you can keep up without missing good information.

③ **Maintain good posture. Avoid slouching.**
Sit upright with your feet planted firmly on the ground and your palms on your thighs. Beware of the impulse to slouch, cross your arms, or lean against your neighbor, as these can encourage drowsiness.

④ **Listen for the law.**
You may feel an emotional pinch when the preacher names the sinner in you. Pay attention to your reaction, and try to focus on waiting for the gospel rather than becoming defensive.

⑤ **Listen for the gospel.**
Many sermons consist of "points" that follow each other as "one," "two," "three." Concentrate on the main heading of the point as you hear the pastor preach on each segment of the sermon. Other times, sermons follow more of a narrative or story approach. Keep your mind engaged to follow the flow of thought or the major ideas that emerge in the sermon.

6 Review.

If you've taken written notes, read through them later that day or the next day and consider corresponding with the preacher if you have questions or need clarification. If you've taken mental notes, review them in a quiet moment. Consider sharing this review time with others in your congregation or household on a weekly basis.

HOW TO RESPOND TO A DISRUPTION DURING WORSHIP

Disruptions during worship are inevitable. The goal is to soften their impact.

❶ Simply ignore the offending event, if possible. Many disruptions are brief and the persons involved act quickly to quiet them. Avoid embarrassing others; maintain your attention on the worship activity.

❷ Some disruptions cannot be ignored and may threaten to continue indefinitely. The agony will go on unless you act. Consider the following types:

Active Children

- *Your Problem:* You are most familiar with your own family. If you sense an outburst will end quickly, simply allow it to pass. If not, escort the child to the lobby for a little quiet time, then return.

Try to ignore worship interruptions you think will end soon.

Note: Under all circumstances, children should be made to feel welcome in worship!

- *Someone Else's Problem:* Politely offer to help, perhaps by helping to occupy the child quietly or—with the parents' permission—by escorting the tot to the lobby, nursery, or cry room.

Personal Electronics

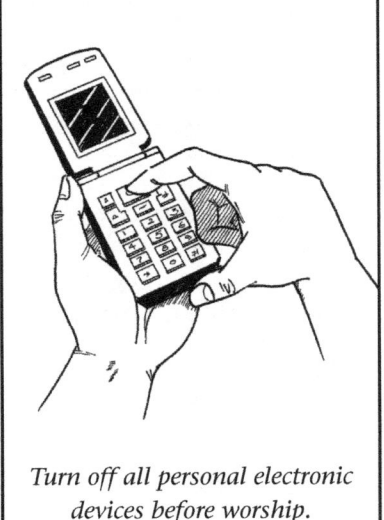

Turn off all personal electronic devices before worship.

- *Your Problem:* Turn off cell phones, pagers, and other electronic alarms immediately and discreetly. If contact is made and it is critical, remove yourself to the lobby and call back. Under no circumstances should you answer your phone during worship.
- *Someone Else's Problem:* Politely ask them to respect worship by moving the conversation to the lobby.

Chatty Neighbor

- *Your Problem:* Chatty persons should be alert to stares and grim looks from neighbors and be prepared to stop talking upon seeing them.
- *Someone Else's Problem:* Politely ask the talkers to wait until after worship to conclude the conversation. During the coffee hour, approach them with a cookie to mend any offense they may have felt.

Cameras
- *Your Problem:* Ask first if cameras are allowed. If so, unobtrusively and discreetly position yourself out of the line of sight of other worshipers. Minimize any potential noise and turn off the flash.
- *Someone Else's Problem:* Politely offer to show the photographer where to stand to get the shot but without obstructing worship.

Sound System Feedback
- Pastors often make jokes to cover for feedback and keep the appropriate mood for worship. If this happens, consider making a donation earmarked for a "new sound system."

Be Aware
- Some people may perceive tennis shoes with light-up soles on acolytes and other worship assistants to be disruptive. If possible, coordinate the color of the shoe lights with the season of the church year to avoid undue flak.

SACRAMENTS

Cumberland Presbyterians celebrate two sacraments in the church. These are baptism and the Lord's Supper.

Sacraments are God's gracious gifts, given by Jesus Christ to the church to establish and nourish our faith.

❶ Sacraments are instituted by Christ.
- Jesus was baptized by John the Baptis; Jesus commanded his disciples to baptize others (Matthew 28:16–20).
- Jesus commanded his disciples to celebrate the last meal he shared with them (1 Corinthians 11:23–26).

❷ Sacraments are available to all persons.
- Marriage is not a sacrament because not everyone is married.
- Ordination is not a sacrament because not everyone is ordained into the church's professional ministry.

Sacraments are received by faith. They are "an outward sign of an invisible grace," meaning that we receive the benefits of the sacraments when we believe God's promises to us in Jesus Christ.

THE ANATOMY OF A BAPTISM

Baptism is a sacrament of the church that takes place during a worship service on the Lord's Day. It symbolizes the baptism of the Holy Spirit and marks the entrance into God's covenant family. The promises of God are received by faith through the Holy Spirit and through the water of baptism.

❶ Infant and Younger Children
- Parents as people of faith and members of the congregation present their child for infant baptism.

- Pastors serve as celebrants for baptism and may ask an ordained elder to assist.

- Parents are asked to make promises for the child.

- The congregation is asked to make promises and pledge support for the child.

- The child is baptized with water "in the name of the Father, Son, and Holy Spirit."

- The baptized child may participate in the sacrament of the Lord's Supper.

❷ Adult and Older Children
- Persons who desire to be baptized may be presented to the congregation by a session member.

- The person expresses the desire to be baptized and confesses faith in Jesus Christ as Lord and Savior, promising to be his faithful disciple.

- The person is baptized with water "in the name of the Father, Son, and Holy Spirit."

- The person is received as a member of the church.

HOW TO RECEIVE THE LORD'S SUPPER

The sacrament of the Lord's Supper is a central act of worship in Cumberland Presbyterian churches. It is an outward and visible sign and seal of the promises God makes in the gospel of Jesus Christ. These promises are received by faith as church members eat the bread and drink the wine, representing Jesus' body and blood (1 Corinthians 11:23–26). The Lord's Supper nourishes the faith of believers in the community and unites Cumberland Presbyterians with all other Christians.

- The Lord's Supper is also called Communion or the Eucharist.
- The "elements" of the Lord's Supper are the bread and the wine.

    The bread may be served from a loaf or in individual pieces; some churches use communion wafers.

    The wine (usually grape juice) may be served from a common chalice or individual cups.

❶ Key Ideas in the Lord's Supper

1. **Covenant.** We join others in the church as the people of God who have received the "new covenant" in Jesus Christ (1 Corinthians 11:25).

2. **Remembrance.** We remember Jesus' death and resurrection (1 Corinthians 11:24) and by faith receive the benefits of all that Jesus has done for us (John 6:53–58).

3. **Reign of God.** We celebrate the return of Jesus and the coming reign of God (1 Corinthians 11:26).

❷ Different Ways of Celebrating the Lord's Supper.
  1. Elders distribute the bread and wine; we receive the elements and pass them to the person next to us.

  2. The congregation proceeds to the front of the church and receives the elements from a pastor or an elder. Then,

     • the bread and the wine may be received separately.

     • the bread may be dipped into a cup of wine (called "intinction").

  3. Groups from the congregation may proceed to tables in the front of the church and be served the elements.

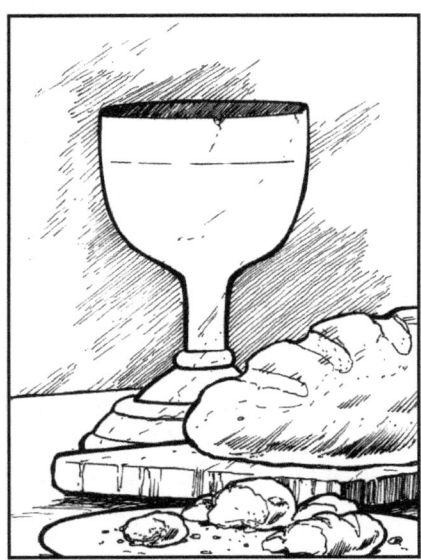

SIX QUESTIONS AND ANSWERS ABOUT THE LORD'S SUPPER

1. **Q.** Why are there different names for the sacrament of the Lord's Supper?

   A. Each name emphasizes a different aspect of the sacrament.

   - Lord's Supper. Reminds us of the Last Supper that Jesus shared with his disciples (Matthew 26:26–29; Mark 14:22–26; Luke 22:14–23).

   - Eucharist. From the Latin word meaning "thanksgiving." We give thanks in the sacrament, just as Jesus did (1 Corinthians 11:24).

   - Communion. Reminds us that we share together the body and blood of Christ and are united with Christ and one another (1 Corinthians 10:16).

2. **Q.** How often do Cumberland Presbyterians celebrate the Lord's Supper?

   A. It varies. Traditionally, American Presbyterians had Communion four times a year. Now many Cumberland Presbyterian churches celebrate the sacrament once a month. Every church session decides the practice for its respective congregation.

3. **Q.** Why do the elders serve Communion to the people in Cumberland Presbyterian churches?

   Note: The word *intinction* is from the Latin word *intingere*, which means "to dip."

A. Elders are representatives of the people of the congregation. They receive the bread and the wine from the pastor, who represents Christ, and distribute them to the people of the congregation. In the pews, we receive the elements and pass them to the person next to us, our "neighbor."

4. Q. Why may baptized children receive the Lord's Supper in Cumberland Presbyterian churches?

A. Baptized children have been received into the "household of God," the "fellowship of the church" in baptism. They receive the bread and the wine in the Lord's Supper because they are "children of the covenant" and have been instructed on the meaning of the sacrament as a sign and seal of God's love in Jesus Christ.

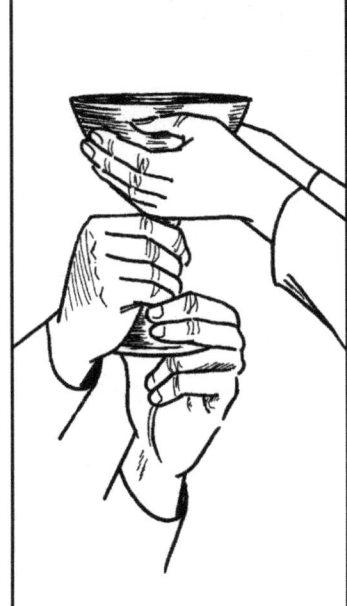

Use teamwork to receive the wine by common cup.

5. Q. Do Cumberland Presbyterians believe that the bread and the wine "turn into" the body and blood of Christ?

A. No. We believe that the elements in Communion are blessed by God to be used to symbolize or represent God's love for us in Christ. We do not believe that the bread and wine are "transformed" physically or in any other way. They are the means God uses to make the message of the gospel of Jesus Christ visible to us.

6. **Q.** Who may participate in the Lord's Supper in Cumberland Presbyterian churches?

   A. Cumberland Presbyterians invite all those who have faith in Jesus Christ and have been baptized to participate in the sacrament of the Lord's Supper. You do not have to be a Cumberland Presbyterian or belong to the local church where the sacrament is being celebrated. Communion nourishes the faith of those who share a common confession of faith in Jesus Christ as their Lord and Savior.

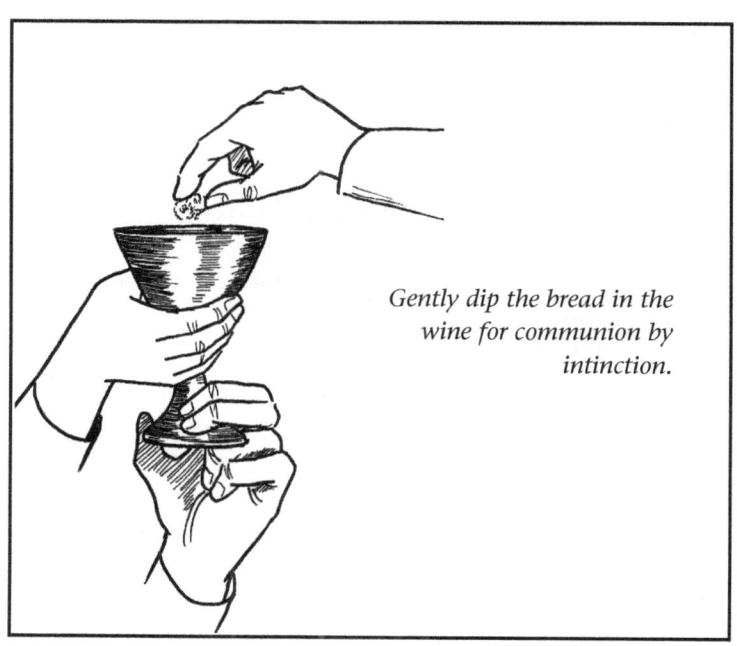

Gently dip the bread in the wine for communion by intinction.

HOW TO PASS THE PLATE

Passing the offering plate requires physical flexibility and an ability to adapt to differing practices. The offering is a practice that dates back to Old Testament times, linking money and personal finance directly to one's identity as a child of God. Giving of one's financial resources is an integral part of a healthy faith life.

❶ Pay close attention to instructions, if any.
The presiding minister may announce the method of offering, or instructions may be printed in the worship bulletin or projected on an overhead screen.

❷ Be alert for the plate's arrival at your row or pew.
Keep an eye on the ushers, if there are any. In most congregations, guiding and safeguarding the offering plate is their job, so wherever they are, so is the plate. As the plate approaches you, set aside other activity and prepare for passing.

❸ Avoid watching your neighbor or making judgments about their offering.
Some people contribute once a month by mail and others by automatic withdrawal from a bank account. If your neighbor passes the plate to you without placing an envelope, check, or cash in it, do not assume they didn't contribute.

❹ Place your offering in the plate as you pass it politely to the next person.
Do not attempt to make change from the plate if your offering is in cash. Avoid letting the plate rest in your lap as you finish writing a check. Simply pass it on and

hand your check to an usher as you leave at the end of worship.

❺ Be sensitive to idiosyncrasies in plate types.
Some congregations use traditional, wide-rimmed, felt-lined, brass-plated offering plates. Some use baskets of varying types.

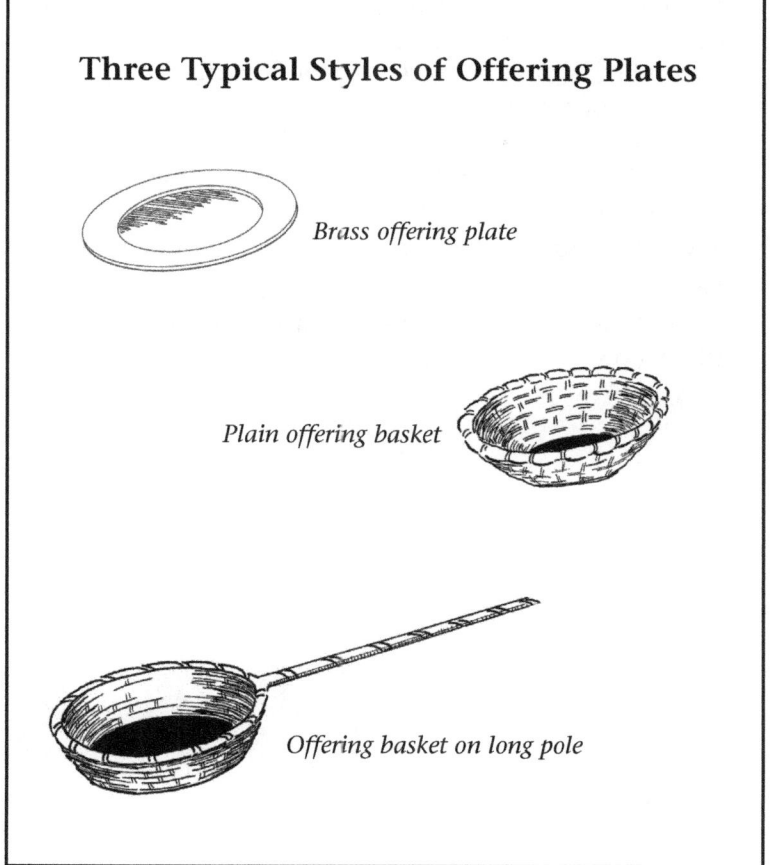

Three Typical Styles of Offering Plates

Brass offering plate

Plain offering basket

Offering basket on long pole

Church Stuff 43

Be Aware

- Some congregations may place the offering plate or basket at the rear of the worship space.
- Your church offering may be tax deductible, as provided by law. Consider making your offering by check or automatic withdrawal; you will receive a statement from your church in the first quarter of the next year.
- Churches often depend entirely upon the money that comes in through congregational offerings. If you are a member, resolve to work yourself toward tithing as a putting-your-money-where-your-mouth-is expression of faith. (The term *tithing* means "one-tenth" and refers to the practice of giving 10 percent of one's gross income to support the church's work.)
- Everyone, regardless of their age, has something to offer.
- Offerings are not fees or dues given out of obligation. They are gifts of thanksgiving returned to God from the heart.

HOW TO SHARE THE PEACE IN CHURCH

In Romans 16:16, Paul tells members of the congregation to "greet one another with a holy kiss." The First Letter of Peter ends, "Greet one another with a kiss of love. Peace to all of you who are in Christ" (1 Peter 5:14).

Some Cumberland Presbyterians worry about this part of the worship service due to its free-for-all nature. Some also feel uncomfortable because of their fear of being hugged. You can survive the peace, however, with these steps.

❶ Adopt a peaceful frame of mind.
Clear your mind of distracting and disrupting thoughts so you can participate joyfully and reverently.

❷ Determine the appropriate form of safe touch.
Handshaking is most common. Be prepared, however, for hugs, half-hugs, one-armed hugs, pats, and other forms of physical contact. Nods are appropriate for distances greater than two pews or rows.

❸ Refrain from extraneous chitchat.
The sharing of the peace is not the time for lengthy introductions, comments about the weather, or observations about yesterday's game. A brief encounter is appropriate, but save conversations for the coffee hour.

❹ Make appropriate eye contact.
Look the other person in the eye but do not stare. The action of looking the person in the eye highlights the relationship brothers and sisters in Christ have with one another.

Make good eye contact as you share God's peace with others.

❺ Declare the peace of God.
"The peace of the Lord be with you," "Peace be with you," "The peace of God," "God's peace," and "The peace of Christ," are ways of speaking the peace. Once spoken, the peace is there. Move on to the next person.

Be Aware
- Safe touch involves contact that occurs within your personal space but does not cause discomfort or unease.

HOW TO STAY ALERT IN CHURCH

❶ Get adequate sleep.
Late Saturday nights are Sunday morning's worst enemy. Resolve to turn in earlier. A good night's sleep on Friday night is equally important to waking rested on Sunday, as sleep debt builds up over time.

❷ Drink plenty of water, though not too much.
It is easier to remain alert when you are well hydrated. One quick bathroom break is considered permissible. Two or more are bad form.

❸ Eat a high-protein breakfast.
Foods high in carbohydrates force your body to metabolize them into sugars, which can make you drowsy. If your diet allows, eat foods high in protein instead, such as bacon and scrambled eggs, with or without cheese.

❹ Arrive early and find the coffee pot.
If you don't drink coffee, consider a caffeinated soda.

❺ Focus on your posture.
Sit up straight with your feet planted firmly on the floor. Avoid slouching, as this encourages sleepiness. Good posture will promote an alert bearing and assist in paying attention, so you'll get more out of worship.

❻ If you have difficulty focusing on the service, divert your attention. Occupy your mind, not your hands.
Look around the worship space for visual stimuli. Keep your mind active in this way while continuing to listen.

❼ Stay alert by flexing muscle groups in a pattern.
Clench toes and feet; flex calf muscles, thighs, glutei, abdomen, hands, arms, chest, and shoulders. Repeat. Avoid shaking, rocking, or other movements that clue others into the fact that you are fighting a nap.

❽ If all else fails, consider pinching yourself.
Dig your nails into the fleshy part of your arm or leg, pinch yourself, bite down on your tongue with moderate pressure. Try not to cry out.

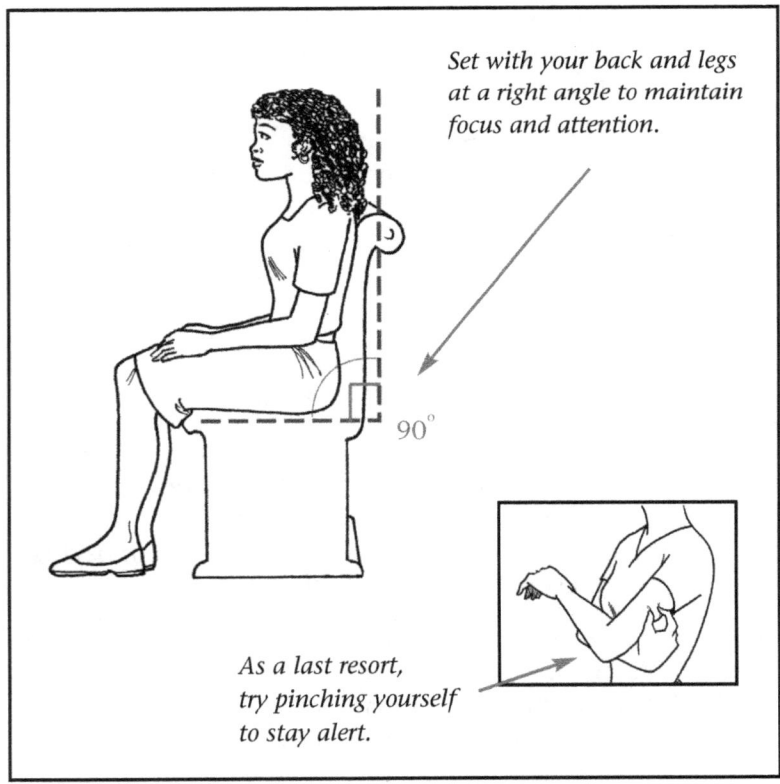

Set with your back and legs at a right angle to maintain focus and attention.

As a last resort, try pinching yourself to stay alert.

WHAT TO BRING TO A CHURCH POTLUCK (BY REGION)

It is a generally followed practice in North American churches to enjoy three courses at potlucks (commonly referred to as "dishes"). Many of these dishes take on the flavor of the regions or cultures they represent. For best results, the preparer should understand the context in which the "dish" is presented.

The Salad

Potluck salads are quite different from actual salads. In preparation for making a potluck salad, ask yourself three questions:

- Is this dish mostly meat-free?
- Can this dish be served with a spoon or salad tongs?
- Can it be served chilled?

If the answer is "yes" to any of these questions, consider the dish a potluck-eligible salad.

The Mixture

This is the foundation of any potluck salad. It gives the salad a sense of direction. If at all possible, use ingredients that are indigenous to your area. For example, broccoli, lettuce, apples, and macaroni are common in more temperate climates.

The Crunchy Stuff

This component gives life and pizzazz to an otherwise bland salad. Examples: tortilla chips, shoestring potato crisps, onion crisps, and fried pigskins.

The Glue

The glue holds the salad together. The variety of available types is stunning, ranging from a traditional oil-based salad dressing to mayonnaise and non-dairy whipped topping. Use your imagination. Consult regional recipes for exact ingredients.

Note: Some salads are best when made well in advance and allowed to sit overnight. This is called *marinating*, or "controlled decomposition." Do not use actual glue adhesive. Other salads are best prepared immediately before serving.

The Casserole

A three-layered dish, typically. In order to make each casserole as culturally relevant as possible, use the following guidelines. Consult local restaurants for ideas, when in doubt.

Starch

East Coast: pasta or rice pilaf

Midwest: rice, potatoes, noodles, or more rice

South: grits

Southwest: black, red, or pinto beans

West Coast: tofu

Meat

East Coast: sausage or pheasant

Midwest: ground beef—in a pinch, SPAM® luncheon meat

South: crawdad or marlin

Southwest: pulled pork

West Coast: tofu

Cereal

East Coast: corn flakes

Midwest: corn flakes

South: corn flakes

Southwest: corn flakes

West Coast: tofu flakes

Note: The starch and meat may be mixed with a cream-based soup. The cereal must always be placed on the top of the casserole.

Salad

Casserole

Dessert

The Dessert

The most highly valued dish at a potluck, this can be the simplest and most fun to make. There are two key ingredients:

1. flour
2. fudge

Regional influences can be quite profound. The following are examples of typical desserts around the country. Consult your church's seniors for the nuances of your region.

Cleveland: fudge brownies with fudge frosting

Kansas City: triple-fudge fudge with fudge sauce and a side of fudge

Los Angeles: tofu fudge

Miami: fudge

New York City: cheesecake with fudge drizzle

Be Aware

- Use caution when preparing a dish. Adding local ingredients to any salad, casserole, or dessert can increase the fellowship factor of your potluck exponentially. It also raises the risk of a "flop."
- Always follow safe food-handling guidelines.
- Any combination of flavored gelatin, shredded carrots, mini-marshmallows, and crushed pineapple is an acceptable "utility" dish, should you be unable to prepare one from the above categories.

CUMBERLAND PRESBYTERIAN ORIGINS

❶ Reformed Churches

Cumberland Presbyterians are part of the whole household of Christians. We are part of the Reformed family of churches. These churches began in the sixteenth century during the Protestant Reformation. They were churches that looked especially to the teachings of Huldrych Zwingli of Zurich (1484–1531) and John Calvin (1509–1564), of Geneva, Switzerland, as reliable ways to understand and interpret the Bible. Other Reformed leaders followed. They wanted to "reform" the Roman Catholic Church on the basis of God's Word in Scripture.

❷ Protestant Churches

Reformed churches became distinguished from Lutheran churches, which followed the teachings of Martin Luther (1483–1546), who had also sought the "reformation" of Catholicism. Reformed churches also followed a different path from those who were known as Anabaptists (today's Baptists, Mennonites, and others) since Anabaptists believed that only adults and not infants should be baptized. Lutheran, Reformed, and Anabaptists are all "Protestants" in that they disagree with the Roman Catholic Church. In England, Anglican churches (Episcopal churches in the U.S. today) emerged as a middle way between Catholicism and Protestantism.

❸ Presbyterian Churches

Presbyterian Churches get their name from their form of church government: government by presbyters or elders.

The primary governing unit is the presbytery, which is composed of clergy and elected lay leaders (elders) in a specific geographical area. The elders who govern in local churches are called the session.

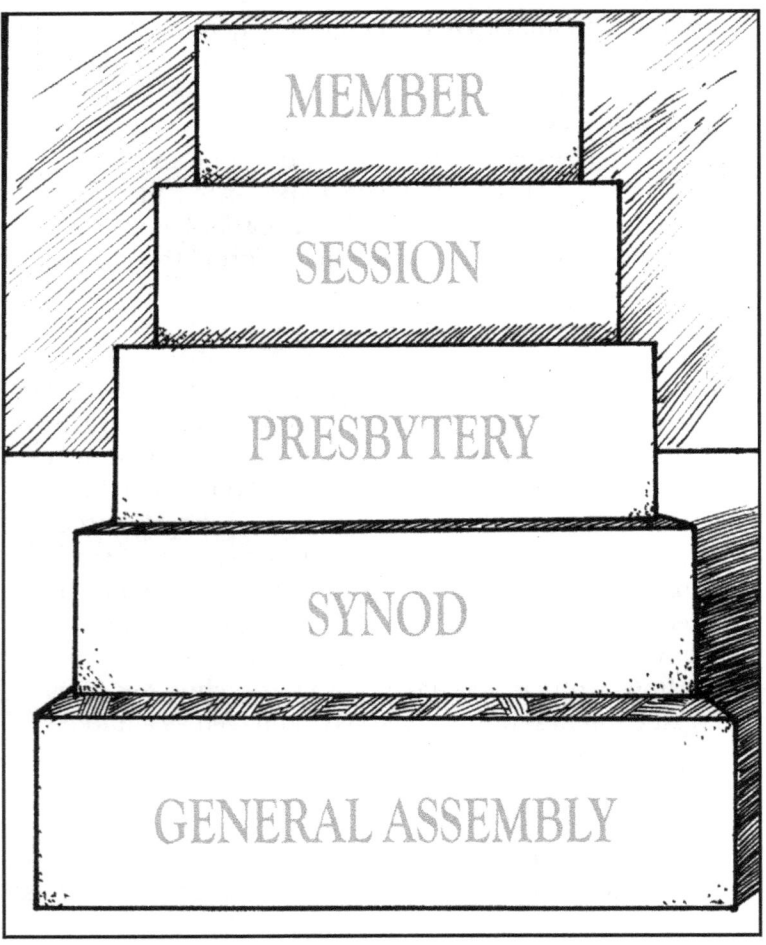

THE PRESBYTERIAN FAMILY IN THE UNITED STATES

Thousands of Presbyterians emigrated from Europe and came to the New World in the seventeenth century and later. Presbyterians were prominent in the country that became the United States during the time of the American Revolution. A Presbyterian clergyman, John Witherspoon, signed the Declaration of Independence.

Today there are a number of Presbyterian denominations in the United States. These emerged from theological differences within the "Presbyterian family."

- Associate Reformed Presbyterian Church
- Bible Presbyterian Church
- Cumberland Presbyterian Church
- Cumberland Presbyterian Church in America
- Evangelical Presbyterian Church
- Orthodox Presbyterian Church
- Presbyterian Church in America
- Presbyterian Church (U.S.A.)
- Reformed Presbyterian Church of North America

BIG-TIME ANCESTORS & LEADERS FOR CUMBERLAND PRESBYTERIANS

The Cumberland Presbyterian family tree stretches back to the sixteenth century. Important leaders emerged who conveyed their beliefs in ways that attracted followers. These leaders contributed to the resources from which Cumberland Presbyterians today continue to draw.

Milton Bird (1807-1871)
> The Cumberland Presbyterian minister, writer, and editor who led efforts to maintain unity in the denomination during the Civil War. Though opposed to secession, he advocated reasoned moderation and worked to keep a division in the church from echoing that of the broken nation. Bird served as moderator of the General Assembly five times and was Stated Clerk of the General Assembly for many years.

John Calvin (1509–1564)
> The most important theologian in the Reformed family. His *Institutes of the Christian Religion* (1536) provided a comprehensive statement of Christian belief. Calvin was highly influential through his biblical commentaries, sermons, letters, and theological tracts. He focused on the greatness of God and God's electing love in Christ who calls the church to be his faithful disciples in this world.

Finis Ewing (1773-1841)
> A Presbyterian minister, a leader in the Great Revival Movement, and "father" of the Cumberland Presbyterian Church. Ewing supported adapting ordination requirements to provide more ministers to preach the Gospel on the American frontier. He focused on the availability

of God's saving grace to all who respond to Jesus Christ in love, putting him at odds with the theology of predestination as taught in the *Westminster Confession*. Together with Samuel McAdow and Samuel King, Ewing constituted Cumberland Presbytery on February 4, 1810. His *Lectures on the Most Important Subjects in Divinity* was an influential early work on Cumberland Presbyterian theology.

John Knox (ca. 1514–1572)
The Scottish reformer who met Calvin in Geneva and then returned to Scotland to become the leading preacher and writer. Knox faced many dangers from his conflicts with the English government officials, most notably, Mary Queen of Scots. He helped write The Scots Confession (1560), a statement of belief that stresses that God alone saves people through Jesus Christ and draws them into the church.

Louisa Woosley (1862-1952)
The first woman ordained to the ministry by any Presbyterian denomination and the second ordained woman in any church of the Reformed family. Woosley was ordained by Nolin Presbytery of the Cumberland Presbyterian Church in 1889. Though Kentucky Synod balked at her ordination, it eventually withstood all challenges. In 1891, Woosley wrote *Shall Woman Preach*, a vigorous, often wry, defense of women's ordination.

Huldrych Zwingli (1484–1531)
The leader who began the Protestant Reformation in Zurich by his lectures and sermons and who vigorously enacted his religious and political views against the reigning Roman Catholic powers. Zwingli's "Sixty-seven Theses" was his statement of belief, grounded, he maintained, in the gospel of Jesus Christ.

FIVE FACTS ABOUT LIFE IN MEDIEVAL TIMES

❶ It lasted more than 1,000 years.
By some counts, the medieval period (or Middle Ages) covered an era that began around the year 391 (when Christianity became the Roman Empire's only legal religion) and ended around 1517 (the year Martin Luther wrote the Ninety-five Theses).

❷ Life was nasty, brutish, and short.
People who survived childhood usually did not live long past age 40. If disease or starvation didn't get you, violence and warfare did. It's been estimated that during the 1400s about one-third of Europe's population died of bubonic plague. Sanitation was practically non-existent.

Road travel was harsh and sanitation was minimal during the Middle Ages.

❸ The Christian church grew larger, more influential, and more dominant.
Headquartered in Rome, the Western church became a superpower. Church and state became inseparable. At its height (ca. 1000–1300), "Christian Crusaders" battled with Muslims and others for control of the "Holy Land," Thomas Aquinas wrote his *Summa Theologica*, and hundreds of "heretics" were burned to death.

❹ The "Cult of the Saints" developed.
Over the centuries, a system grew in which the leftover good works (merits) of the saints could be distributed to others, with the pope in charge of this store (treasury) of good works. With his Ninety-five Theses, Luther challenged this system.

❺ Humanist and Renaissance-age thinkers also worked for reform.
At the end of the Middle Ages, early reformers such as Jan Hus and Girolamo Savonarola confronted the church corruptions they saw. Hus was burned, and Savonarola was hanged. For other examples, see "History's Six Most Notorious Heretics" on the next two pages.

HISTORY'S SIX MOST NOTORIOUS HERETICS

Though vilified by those who write history, heretics played a critical role in the church. They refined its message and forced the church to be honest with itself. But heretics usually paid the ultimate price, and often they were wrong.

❶ Hypatia of Alexandria (370–415)
Hypatia was an African philosopher, mathematician, physicist, astronomer, and director of Alexandria's Library, once the largest in the world. Bishop Cyril of Alexandria, out of jealousy, declared her a heretic and ordered her to be tortured and burned at the stake, together with her writings. Her mistakes were to prefer study to marriage, to know more than the bishop, and to be a female teacher of males.

❷ Pelagius (354–418)
Pelagius was a Celtic monk who believed in the goodness of human nature and the freedom of human will. These beliefs led him to denounce the doctrine of original sin—a core tenet of the church—and suggest that human beings were equal participants in their salvation with Jesus Christ. When Pelagius taught that one could achieve grace without the church, he was excommunicated.

❸ Joan of Arc (1412–1431)
Joan was a French peasant girl who was able to hear heavenly voices that urged her to liberate her nation from the British occupation. She was 19 when sentenced as a heretic and burned at the stake. Joan's fault was to be a better army leader than men. She is now a national hero.

④ Girolamo Savonarola (1452–1498)
His parents wanted him to be a physician, but this Italian youngster decided to be a Dominican monk and serve people who were poor. He preached against Pope Alexander VI and the powerful Medici family. Members of the wealthy church and society hung and burned him, then threw his ashes in the Arnos River to prevent him from having a restful place.

⑤ Martin Luther (1483–1546)
His father, a peasant and coal miner, wanted him to be a lawyer. Martin disappointed him and became an Augustinian monk. Emperor Charles V and Pope Leo X threw him out of the church and put a price on his head, but Luther continued serving the poor, preaching and living the Bible, and sharing hospitality at the family dinner table.

⑥ Hatuey (?–1511)
This Native American leader from the Guahaba region escaped from Haiti to Cuba. The brave Hatuey was captured and declared a heretic. A priest wanted to baptize him in order for the Indian to get to heaven after being burnt. The Taíno chief rejected the Christian rite when he heard that in heaven there would also be people from Spain.

HOW TO AVOID GETTING BURNED AT THE STAKE

Burning at the stake has a centuries-long history as punishment for heretics. (A *heretic* is someone who challenges established church teachings.) Some historians argue that many heretics have performed an essential function by forcing the church to clarify its position.

Martin Luther himself was declared a heretic by the pope in 1521, when he would not recant his teachings, but he survived under the protection of a friendly prince. While heretics are no longer treated in this way, it is nevertheless good to be prepared.

❶ Avoid public heresy.
Heresy is any formal public statement that disagrees with the church on an issue of dogma. The Lutheran church was founded upon such statements. Martin Luther's Ninety-five Theses, for example, were heretical and entered as evidence at the Diet of Worms in 1521.

Here's what to do if you are accused of heresy:

- Demand an immediate public trial. By this point, your rights may have evaporated. Speak up anyway.

- State your position clearly and repeatedly. Get it on the record in your own words.

- Consider your options. If in a church trial you believe you might change enough minds to ward off execution, consider proceeding.

If accused of heresy, demand an immediate public trial. State your position clearly.

- Support your case with Holy Scripture. In a trial, you will be doomed without sufficient evidence from the Bible, history, and church doctrine.

- If the above steps fail, consider recanting. You could be wrong.

❷ Avoid practicing witchcraft.
Witchcraft is considered a form of heresy, since it depends upon powers other than God and the authority of the church. Practicing witchcraft does *not* include wearing Halloween costumes or reading books about wizards.

❸ Avoid getting nabbed in a political uprising.
Historically, persons who posed a political threat were sometimes burned at the stake. Or crucified.

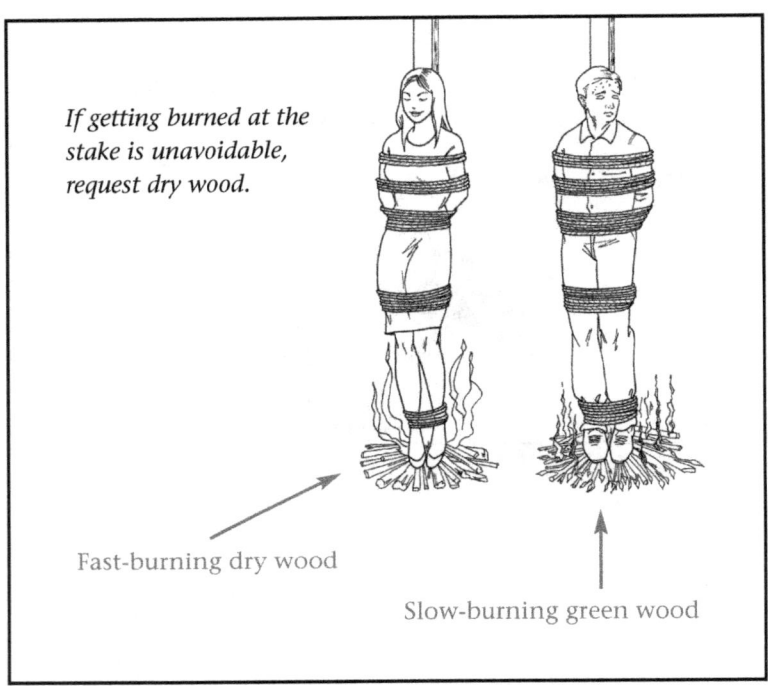

If getting burned at the stake is unavoidable, request dry wood.

Fast-burning dry wood

Slow-burning green wood

Be Aware

- If you find yourself in a situation where being burned at the stake poses an imminent threat, try wearing flame-retardant material.
- If there is no hope of escape, request dry wood and plenty of dry kindling. Green wood burns slower, smokier, and at lower temperatures, causing a more painful death.

WORLD RELIGIONS

Listed by approximate number of adherents:

Christianity	2 billion
Islam	1.3 billion
Hinduism	900 million
Agnostic/Atheist/Non-Religious	850 million
Buddhism	360 million
Confucianism and Chinese traditional	225 million
Primal-indigenous	150 million
African traditional	95 million
Sikhism	23 million
Juche	19 million
Judaism	14 million
Spiritism	14 million
Baha'i	7 million
Jainism	4 million
Shinto	4 million
Cao Dai	3 million
Tenrikyo	2.4 million
Neo-Paganism	1 million
Unitarian-Universalism	800,000
Rastafarianism	700,000
Scientology	600,000
Zoroastrianism	150,000

COMPARATIVE RELIGIONS

	Baha'i	Buddhism	Christianity
Founder and date founded	Bahá'u'lláh (1817-1892) founded Babism in 1844 from which Baha'i grew.	Founded by Siddhartha Gautama (the Buddha) in Nepal in the 6th-5th centuries B.C.	Founded by Jesus of Nazareth, a Palestinian Jew, in the early 1st century A.D.
Number of adherents in 2000	About 7 million worldwide; 750,000 U.S.	360 million worldwide; 2 million U.S.	About 2 billion worldwide; 160 million U.S.
Main tenets	The oneness of God, the oneness of humanity, and the common foundation of all religion. Also, equality of men and women, universal education, world peace, and a world federal government.	Meditation and the practice of virtuous and moral behavior can lead to *Nirvana*, the state of enlightenment. Before that, one is subjected to repeated lifetimes, based on behavior.	Jesus is the Son of God and God in human form. In his death and resurrection, he redeems humanity from sin and gives believers eternal life. His teachings frame the godly life for his followers.
Sacred or primary writing	Bahá'u'lláh's teachings, along with those of the Bab, are collected and published.	The Buddha's teachings and wisdom are collected and published.	The Bible is a collection of Jewish and Near Eastern writings spanning some 1,400 years.

Confucianism	Hinduism	Islam	Judaism
Founded by the Chinese philosopher Confucius in the 6th-5th centuries B.C. One of several traditional Chinese religions.	Developed in the 2nd century B.C. from indigenous religions in India, and later combined with other religions, such as Vaishnavism.	Founded by the prophet Muhammad ca. A.D. 610. The word *Islam* is Arabic for "submission to God."	Founded by Abraham, Isaac, and Jacob ca. 2000 B.C.
6 million worldwide (does not include other traditional Chinese beliefs); U.S. uncertain.	900 million worldwide; 950,000 U.S.	1.3 billion worldwide; 5.6 million U.S.	14 million worldwide; 5.5 million U.S.
Confucius's followers wrote down his sayings or *Analects*. They stress relationships between individuals, families, and society based on proper behavior and sympathy.	Hinduism is based on a broad system of sects. The goal is release from repeated reincarnation through yoga, adherence to the Vedic scriptures, and devotion to a personal guru.	Followers worship Allah through the Five Pillars. Muslims who die believing in God, and that Muhammad is God's messenger, will enter Paradise.	Judaism holds the belief in a monotheistic God, whose Word is revealed in the Hebrew Bible, especially the Torah. Jews await the coming of a messiah to restore creation.
Confucius's *Analects* are collected and still published.	The Hindu scriptures and Vedic texts.	The Koran is a collection of Muhammad's writings.	The Hebrew scriptures compose the Christian Old Testament.

FAMILY TREE OF CHRISTIANITY

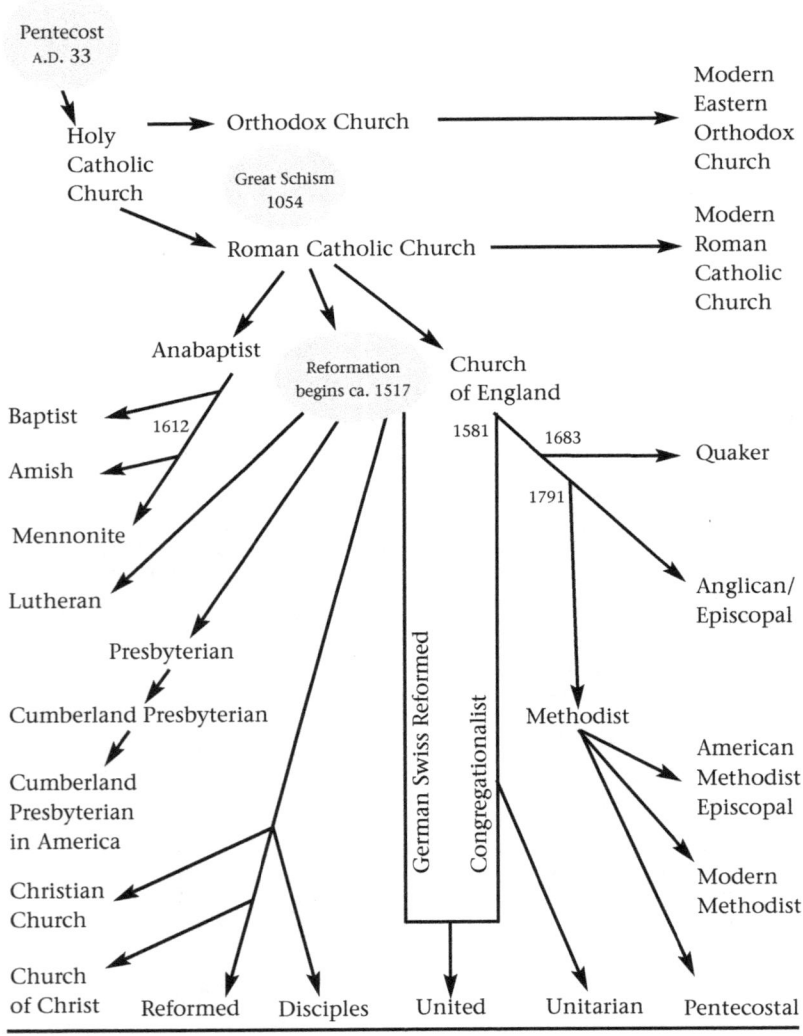

U.S. CHRISTIAN DENOMINATIONS

Listed by approximate number of adult adherents:

Catholic	60 million
Baptist	30 million
Methodist/Wesleyan	13 million
Lutheran	9 million
Pentecostal/Charismatic	5 million
Orthodox	4 million
Presbyterian	4 million
Episcopalian/Anglican	3 million
Churches of Christ	3 million
Congregational/ United Church of Christ	2 million
Assemblies of God	1 million
Adventist	100,000
Cumberland Presbyterian	80,000

COMPARATIVE DENOMINATIONS:

	Lutheran	Catholic	Orthodox
Founded when and by whom?	1517: Martin Luther challenges Catholic teachings with his Ninety-five Theses. 1530: the Augsburg Confession is published.	Catholics consider Jesus' disciple Peter (died ca. A.D. 66) the first pope. Through Gregory the Great (540-604), papacy is firmly established.	A.D 330: Emperor Constantine renames Byzantium "Constantinople" and declares Christianity the empire's religion.
Adherents in 2000?	About 60 million worldwide; about 9 million U.S.	About 1 billion worldwide; 60 million U.S.	About 225 million worldwide; about 4 million U.S.
How is Scripture viewed?	Protestant canon contains 39 OT books, 27 NT. Scripture alone is the authoritative witness to the gospel.	The canon is 46 books in the OT (Apocrypha included) and 27 in the NT. Interpretation is subject to church tradition.	49 OT books (Catholic plus three more) and 27 NT. Scripture is subject to tradition.
How are we saved?	We are saved by grace when God grants righteousness through faith alone. Good works inevitably result, but they are not the basis of salvation.	God infuses the gift of faith in the baptized, which is maintained by good works and receiving Penance and the Eucharist.	God became human so humans could be deified, that is, have the energy of God's life in them.
What is the church?	The congregation of believers, mixed with the lost, in which the gospel is preached and the sacraments are administered.	The mystical body of Christ, who Catholics believe established it with the pope as its head; he pronounces doctrine infallibly.	The body of Christ in unbroken historical connection with the apostles; the Roman pope is one of many patriarchs who govern.
What about the sacraments?	Baptism is necessary for salvation. The Lord's Supper is bread & wine that, with God's Word are truly Jesus' body & blood.	Catholics hold seven sacraments. Baptism removes original sin; usually infants. The Eucharist undergoes transubstantiation.	Baptism initiates God's life in the baptized adults and children. In the Eucharist, bread & wine are changed into body & blood.

The Cumberland Presbyterian Handbook

Liturgical Churches

	Anglican	Cumberland Presbyterian	Methodist
Founded when and by whom?	1534: Henry VIII is declared head of the Church of England. 1549: Thomas Cranmer produces the first *Book of Common Prayer*.	1810: Cumberland Presbytery forms as a church body separate from the Presbyterian Church	1738: Anglican ministers John and Charles Wesley convert. 1784: U.S. Methodists form a separate church body.
Adherents in 2000?	45-75 million worldwide; about 3 million U.S.	80 thousand worldwide	20-40 million worldwide; about 13 million U.S.
How is Scripture viewed?	Protestant canon accepted. Scripture is interpreted in light of tradition and reason.	Protestant canon accepted. Scripture's authority "is founded on the truth contained in them and the voice of God speaking through them."	Protestant canon accepted. Scripture is primary source for Christian doctrine.
How are we saved?	We share in Christ's victory, who died for our sins, freeing us through baptism to become living members of the church.	We are saved by grace alone. Good works result, but are not the basis of salvation.	We are saved by grace alone. Good works must result, but do not obtain salvation.
What is the church?	The body of Christ is based on "apostolic succession" of bishops, going back to the apostles. In the U.S., it is the Episcopal Church.	The body of Christ includes "all who respond in faith to God's saving grace" and "enter into covenant with God and each other."	The body of Christ, represented by church institutions. Bishops oversee regions and appoint pastors, who are itinerant.
What about the sacraments?	Baptism brings infant and convert initiates into the church; in Communion, Christ's body & blood are truly present.	Baptism is not necessary for salvation. In the Lord's Supper Christ's body & blood are spiritually present to believers.	Baptism is a sign of regeneration; in the Lord's Supper, Jesus is really present.

Church Stuff

COMPARATIVE DENOMINATIONS:

	Anabaptist	Congregational	Baptist
Founded when and by whom?	1523: Protestants in Zurich, Switzerland, begin believers' baptism. 1537: Menno Simons begins Mennonite movement.	1607: Members of England's illegal "house church" exiled. 1620: Congregationalists arrive in the New World on the *Mayflower*.	1612: John Smythe and other Puritans form the first Baptist church. 1639: The first Baptist church in America is established.
Adherents in 2000?	About 2 million worldwide; about 600,000 U.S.	More than 2 million worldwide; about 2 million U.S.	100 million worldwide; about 30 million U.S.
How is Scripture viewed?	Protestant canon accepted. Scripture is inspired but not infallible. Jesus is living Word; Scripture is written Word.	Protestant canon accepted. Bible is the authoritative witness to the Word of God.	Protestant canon accepted. Scripture is inspired and without error; the sole rule of faith.
How are we saved?	Salvation is a personal experience. Through faith in Jesus, we become at peace with God, moving us to follow Jesus' example by being peacemakers.	God promises forgiveness and grace to save "from sin and aimlessness" all who trust him, who accept his call to serve the whole human family.	Salvation is offered freely to all who accept Jesus as Savior. There is no salvation apart from personal faith in Christ.
What is the church?	The body of Christ, the assembly and society of believers. No one system of government is recognized.	The people of God living as Jesus' disciples. Each local church is self-governing and chooses its own ministers.	The body of Christ; the redeemed throughout history. The term *church* usually refers to local congregations, which are autonomous.
What about the sacraments?	Baptism is for believers only. The Lord's Supper is a memorial of his death.	Congregations may practice infant baptism or believers' baptism or both. Sacraments are symbols.	Baptism is immersion of believers, only as a symbol. The Lord's Supper is symbolic.

Non-Liturgical Churches

	Churches of Christ	Adventist	Pentecostal
Founded when and by whom?	1801: Barton Stone holds Cane Ridge Revival in Kentucky. 1832: Stone's Christians unite with Disciples of Christ.	1844: William Miller's prediction of Christ's return that year failed. 1863: Seventh-Day Adventist Church is organized.	1901: Kansas college students speak in tongues. 1906: Azusa Street revival in L.A. launches movement. 1914: Assemblies of God organized.
Adherents in 2000?	5-6 million worldwide; about 3 million U.S.	About 11 million worldwide; about 100,000 U.S.	About 500 million worldwide; about 5 million U.S.
How is Scripture viewed?	Protestant canon accepted. Scripture is the Word of God. Disciples of Christ view it as a witness to Christ, but fallible.	Protestant canon accepted. Scripture is inspired and without error; Ellen G. White, an early leader, was a prophet.	Protestant canon accepted. Scripture is inspired and without error. Some leaders are considered prophets.
How are we saved?	We must hear the gospel, repent, confess Christ, and be baptized. Disciples of Christ: God saves people by grace.	We repent by believing in Christ as Example (in his life) and Substitute (by his death). Those who are found right with God will be saved.	We are saved by God's grace through Jesus, resulting in our being born again in the Spirit, as evidenced by a life of holiness.
What is the church?	The assembly of those who have responded rightly to the gospel; it must be called only by the name of Christ.	Includes all who believe in Christ. The last days are a time of apostasy, when a remnant keeps God's commandments faithfully.	The body of Christ, in which the Holy Spirit dwells; the agency for bringing the gospel of salvation to the whole world.
What about the sacraments?	Baptism is the immersion of believers only, as the initial act of obedience to the gospel. The Lord's Supper is a symbolic memorial.	Baptism is the immersion of believers only. Baptism and the Lord's Supper are symbolic only.	Baptism is immersion of believers only. A further "baptism in the Holy Spirit" is offered. Lord's Supper is symbolic.

Church Stuff

THE SEASONS OF THE CHURCH YEAR AND WHAT THEY MEAN

Advent is a season of longing and anticipation, during which we prepare for the coming of Jesus. The church year begins with Advent, as life begins with birth, starting four Sundays before Christmas. The liturgical color for Advent is either purple or blue, which symbolizes waiting and hope.

Christmas is a day *and* a season when we celebrate God's coming among us as a human child: Jesus, *Emmanuel* (which means "God with us"). The liturgical color for Christmas is white, which reminds us that Jesus is the Light of the world. Christmas lasts for 12 days, from December 25 to January 5.

Epiphany is celebrated on January 6, when we remember the Wise Men's visit to the Christ child. The color for Epiphany Day is white. During the time after Epiphany we hear stories about Jesus' baptism and early ministry. The color for these Sundays is sometimes white and sometimes green. On the last Sunday we celebrate the Transfiguration. The color for this day is white, and we hear the story of Jesus shining brightly on the mountaintop.

Lent is a season when we turn toward God and think about how our lives need to change. This is also a time to remember our baptism, and how that gift gives us a new start every day! The color for Lent is purple, symbolizing repentance. Lent begins on Ash Wednesday and lasts for 40 days (not including Sundays) and ends on the Saturday before Easter Sunday.

The Three Days are the most important part of the Christian calendar because they mark Jesus' last days, death, and resurrection. These days (approximately three 24-hour periods) begin on Maundy Thursday evening and conclude on Easter evening. On *Maundy Thursday* we hear the story of Jesus' last meal with his disciples and his act of service and love in washing their feet. On *Good Friday* we hear of Jesus' trial, crucifixion, death, and burial. On *Saturday*, at the nighttime *Easter Vigil*, we hear stories about the amazing things God has done for us. It is a night of light, Scripture readings, baptismal remembrance, and Communion—the greatest night of the year for Christians. On *Easter Sunday* we celebrate Jesus' resurrection and our new lives in Christ. Easter falls on a different date each year—sometime between March 22 and April 25.

Easter is not just one day, but a whole season when we celebrate the resurrected Jesus. The season begins on Easter Sunday and lasts for 50 days (including Sundays). The color is white, symbolizing resurrection and joy. The Day of Pentecost falls on the 50th day of the season (*Pentecost* means 50th), when we honor the Holy Spirit and the church's mission in the world. This day uses the fiery color of red.

Time after Pentecost is the longest season in the church calendar, lasting almost half the year. Sometimes this is called "ordinary time" because there aren't many special celebrations during these weeks. The liturgical color for the time after Pentecost is green, representing life and growth. Each week we hear a different story about Jesus' ministry from one of the four Gospels.

Special Days and Seasons are celebrated throughout the year. Some days occur the same time each year, such as Reformation Sunday (last Sunday in October). Others, like Baptism of the Lord, Pentecost, and Trinity Sunday, do not.

THE SEASONS OF THE CHURCH YEAR

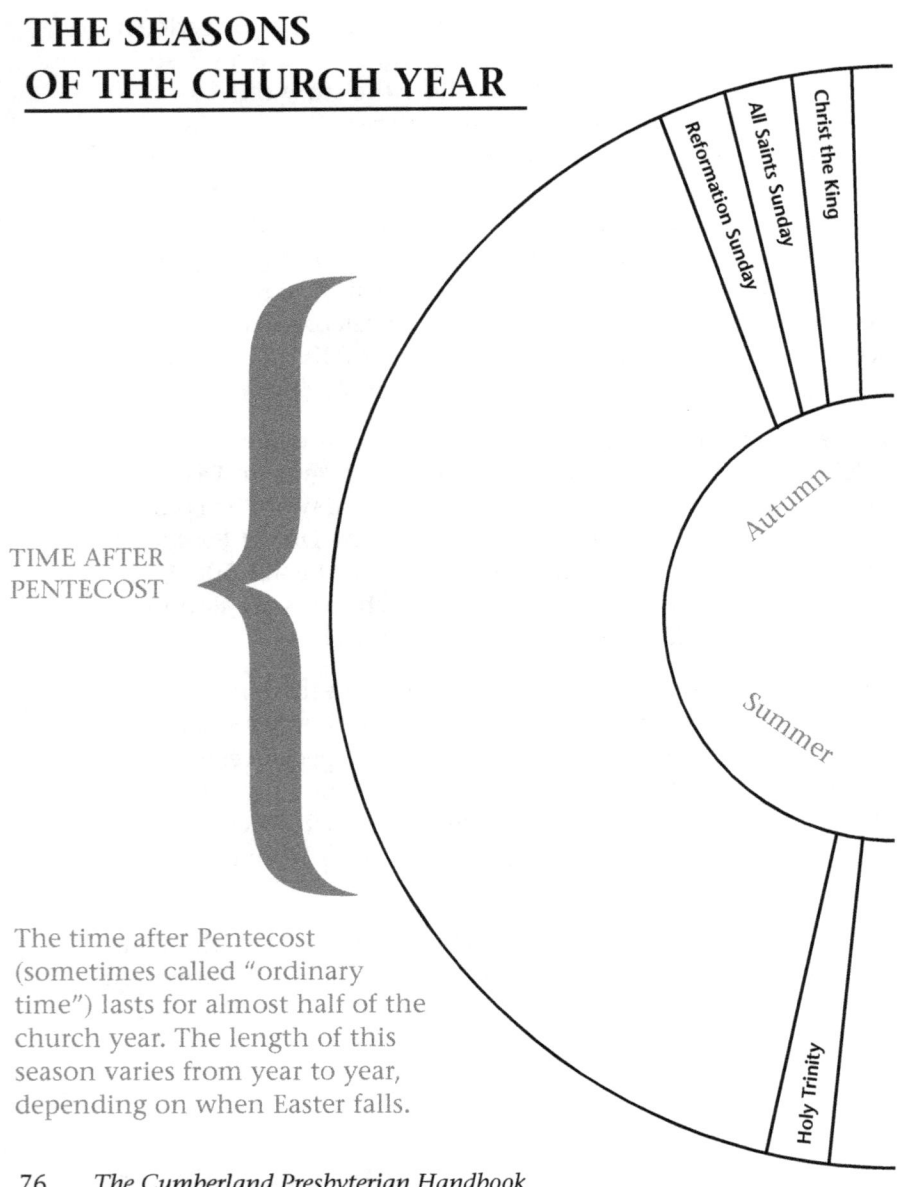

TIME AFTER PENTECOST

The time after Pentecost (sometimes called "ordinary time") lasts for almost half of the church year. The length of this season varies from year to year, depending on when Easter falls.

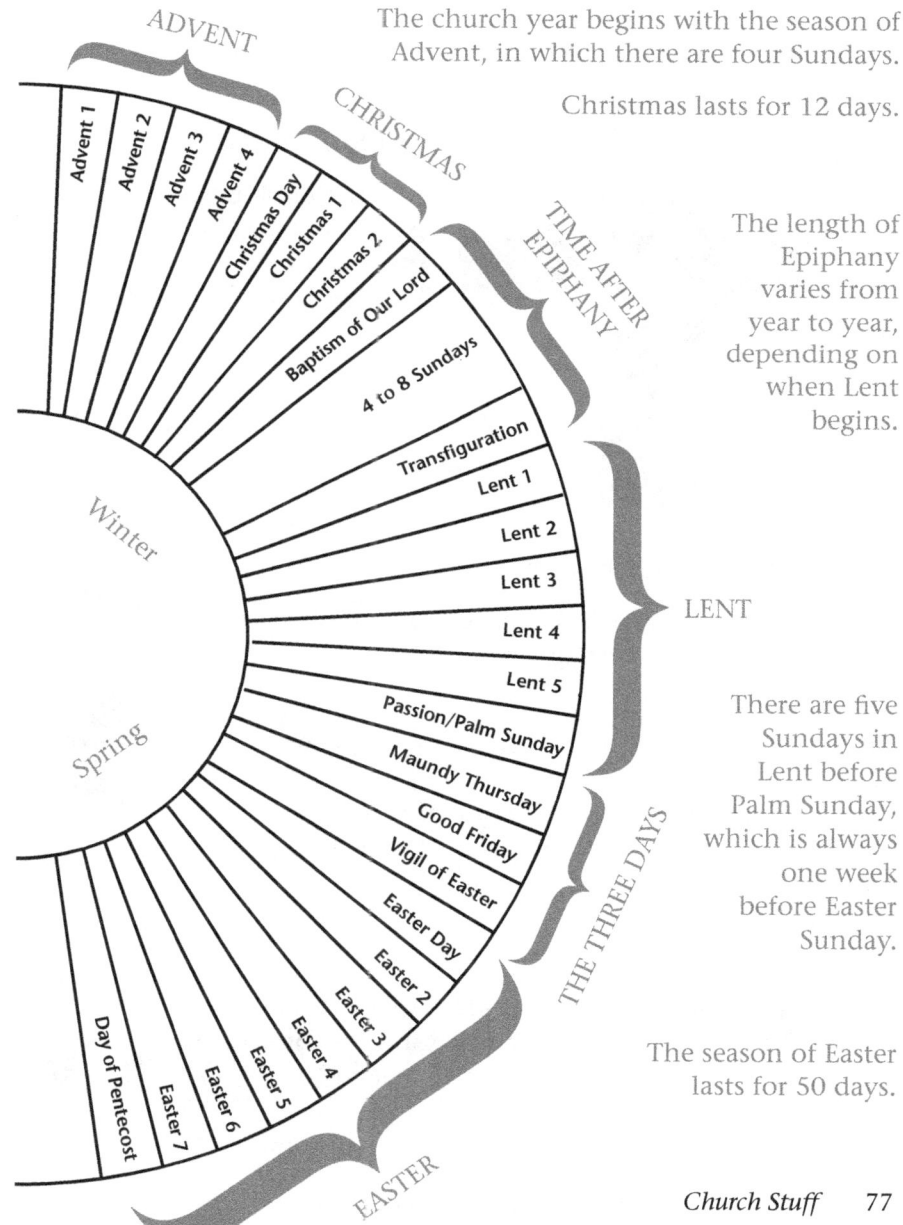

The church year begins with the season of Advent, in which there are four Sundays.

Christmas lasts for 12 days.

The length of Epiphany varies from year to year, depending on when Lent begins.

There are five Sundays in Lent before Palm Sunday, which is always one week before Easter Sunday.

The season of Easter lasts for 50 days.

Church Stuff

Cumberland Presbyterian Symbol

The full symbol

A Celtic cross created by four people forming a circle. The people of God become the Body of Christ in the world.

The component parts

The People   The connectional nature of the church.

The Circle   The people of God form a great circle of love and grace.

The Chalices   The negative space reveals the Cup of Salvation for the world.

EVERYDAY STUFF

Believing in God involves more than going to church and reading the Bible. It's about keeping your faith with you in every part of your life.

This section includes:

- Advice for helping people in times of trouble.
- Tips on forgiving others and treating them with respect—even if you don't always feel like it.
- Information on how to talk to your friends about the Cumberland Presbyterian Church.

HOW TO UNDERSTAND THE RELATIONSHIP BETWEEN THE LAW AND GRACE

Cumberland Presbyterians believe in both the law of God and the grace of God. These themes are found throughout the Bible in both the Old and the New Testament. The law is not confined to the Old Testament; and grace is not confined to the New Testament. Each is found in the whole Bible and each is important for the Christian. Cumberland Presbyterians affirm both as good gifts from God.

① The Purpose of Law

The law of God is expressed in the Ten Commandments (Exodus 20). God gave the *Torah* (Law) to the people of Israel to show them how God wanted them to live. They were not to worship idols, not to steal, to honor their parents, remember the Sabbath day, and so forth. The ceremonial and dietary laws in the Old Testament were the specific forms God desired to help the people live in accord with God's will in obedience. So law is good. The Psalms see the law as a blessing to be loved and treasured. (See Psalm 119.) The people of Israel were to obey God's law as an expression of obedience and gratitude for God's

love and liberation from their slavery in Egypt. The law is introduced by the command to remember that God had saved the people (Exodus 20:2).

❷ The Purpose of the Gospel
The gospel is the "good news" of Jesus Christ. Cumberland Presbyterians believe that God has become a person in Jesus Christ to provide salvation or a restored relationship with God for those who believe in Christ (John 3:1–16). We believe in Jesus Christ by faith, the gift of the Holy Spirit (Ephesians 2:8–9). Human sin has caused a rupture in the relationship God intends to have with humans. Due to sin, humans do not want to obey God's law or seek God's will—we want to live life "my way," instead of "God's way." So God has come in Jesus Christ to provide a way of forgiving sin and reconciling us to the God who created us and loves us. Since we cannot obey God's law and "gain" salvation by our own efforts, God provides a way of salvation in Jesus Christ—and this is the purpose of the gospel.

❸ Law and Gospel; Gospel and Law
Cumberland Presbyterians believe that we receive salvation by God's grace—as an undeserved gift, by faith in Jesus Christ. We do not try to keep the law to gain salvation or a reconciled relationship with God, by "good works." Instead, we believe in Jesus Christ as God's Son who died for our sins (Romans 5:8) and receive the benefits of Christ's life, death, and resurrection. So we are saved by Jesus Christ in the gospel.

But the moral law—the Ten Commandments—still plays a vital role in the Christian life. When we are reconciled to God, we seek to obey God's will as an expression of love and obedience and gratitude to God. We learn God's will through God's law. We see in the law the kind of people God wants us to be. So the law is our guide to living an obedient, faithful Christian life. We obey God's law out of gratitude—not as a means to *gain* salvation, but as an *expression of* salvation. We obey God's law joyfully, in gratitude as we find our salvation in Jesus Christ by faith (Romans 5:1).

HOW TO KNOW WHAT GOD WANTS YOU TO DO WITH YOUR LIFE

One of the biggest questions every Christian faces is: What does God want me to do with my life? Should I simply follow my interests? Should I prepare for the job where I'll make the most money? Does God care what I do?

Cumberland Presbyterians believe God "calls" us to be followers of Jesus Christ and also can "call" us to various forms of work and service so we can live out our discipleship in the world. This is referred to as "vocation" or "calling."

The call to all Christians is to be disciples or followers of Jesus Christ. Just as Jesus called people to follow him during his life, so Christ continues to call us to have faith in him and commit our lives to his service.

We can live out our Christian calling by the kinds of work and service we do during our lives. Our professions or our jobs are ways by which we serve God. Our service in our homes, our communities, and to others are callings through which God is glorified.

When we recognize that we can serve God through who we are and what we do, every day can be exciting! Our work can serve good purposes—God's purposes—in society. Every Christian can be the person God calls us to be. We can use our time, talents, and abilities in the work we do and the relationships we establish to be followers of Jesus Christ. This is what God wants us to do with our lives.

Everyday Stuff

HOW CUMBERLAND PRESBYTERIANS UNDERSTAND EVANGELISM

"Evangelism" comes from the word *evangel,* which means "good news." The "good news" is the gospel of Jesus Christ, which the angels proclaimed when Jesus was born (Luke 2:10).

Cumberland Presbyterians recognize that Christians are called to share the good news of Jesus Christ. We share Christ with people in many ways. Often we use words, talking, writing, preaching, or teaching. Just as often, we use actions. Since Jesus cared for the whole human person, the church shares God's love in Christ through many activities. Among these are:

- Education
- Feeding the hungry
- Healing ministries
- Pastoral care
- Peacemaking
- Caring for the poor
- Working for justice

HOW TO PRAY

Prayer is intimate communication with God and can be used before a meal, at bedtime, during a worship service, or any time the need or opportunity arises. Silent and spoken prayers are both okay and may be used liberally throughout the day. Prayer is also taking time to listen to what God is saying to us. Spontaneous prayer is often best, but the following process may help build the habit.

1. Assess your need for prayer.
   Take stock of the situation at hand, including your motivations. What are you praying *for* and why?

2. Select a type of prayer.
   Prayers of *adoration* (praise to God) *supplication* (requests for God's help), *contrition* (in which sin is confessed and forgiveness requested), *intercession* (on behalf of others), and others are good and time tested. Books of personal prayers, hymnals, and devotionals often contain helpful, prewritten prayers. Consider also an ad-libbed prayer from the heart.

3. Select a physical prayer posture.
   Many postures are appropriate:

   - The most common type of prayer in the New Testament is from a prone position, lying face-down on the ground, arms spread.

   - Kneeling with your face and palms upturned is good for prayers of supplication.

   - Bowed head with closed eyes and hands folded is common today and aids concentration.

   There is no "official" posture for prayer. Choose your posture according to your individual prayer needs.

Everyday Stuff

Choose a comfortable and appropriate prayer posture for your prayer time.

❹ Offer your prayer.
Pray with confidence. God listens to all prayer and responds. Breathe deeply, relax, and be open as the Spirit leads you.

❺ Listen.
Take time during your prayer simply to listen. Some prayer traditions involve only silent meditation as a means of listening for God's voice.

Be Aware

- God hears every prayer. Feel free to take all your feelings and experiences to God in prayer—even the ones you think are not so nice. God can handle it.
- Prayer can be done either alone or in the company of others (corporately).
- Environment matters. If possible, consider lighting a candle and dimming the lights to set the correct mood and help block out distractions.

HOW TO WORK FOR PEACE AND JUSTICE ON BEHALF OF PEOPLE WHO ARE POOR AND OPPRESSED

Cumberland Presbyterians have a long record of working to benefit the poor and oppressed around the world. We remember the example of Jesus whenever we seek to offer ministry to people at the point of their need. Cumberland Presbyterians established schools where we identified a need for education and hunger ministries when the need was for adequate nutrition. Often we partner with other churches and groups to extend our service beyond our borders.

Cumberland Presbyterian congregations set justice as one of their highest priorities, giving time and money both locally and globally. As followers of Jesus Christ, each individual Christian is linked to Jesus' compassion for people who are poor and called to work tirelessly on their behalf, as he did.

1. Include people who are poor and oppressed in your daily prayers.
   Keep the needs of others in mind, especially people who suffer as a result of economic inequality, political oppression, or natural disaster. Name specific situations in your prayers, and use specific place names and people's names whenever possible. Keep the newspaper on your lap as you pray, if necessary.

2. Include people who are poor and oppressed in your personal or household budget.
   Dedicate some of your personal giving to economic-aid organizations. This should include your congregation.

❸ Pay close attention to economic and political conditions in other nations.
You can't help if you don't know what's really going on. Resolve to be a well-informed person who tests the worldview in the news against the worldview in the Bible. Utilize the Internet to locate independent and alternative news sources with unique, on-the-spot perspectives.

❹ Get to know organizations that work for justice locally.
Your congregation probably already organizes to do justice work in your neighborhood. If not, consider taking responsibility to organize a ministry team in your church.

❺ Make working for justice part of your weekly or monthly routine.
Devote a portion of your time regularly to a specific activity that personally connects you to people who are poor and disenfranchised. There is no substitute for personal contact.

❻ Vote your conscience.
If you are of voting age, remember that nations will be judged by the way they treat people who are disadvantaged. Keep this in mind when you go to your polling place.

❼ Advocate for a cause in which you believe, one that has meaning for you personally.

HOW TO IDENTIFY A GENUINE MIRACLE

The term *miracle* describes something that causes wonder. In one sense, as Christians, we should regard everything as a "miracle"! The universe and all that's in it; our lives, our relationships, our needs being met—as people of faith, we see that God's hand has provided everything. We recognize God in all things. So, we say, "It's a miracle!" We live in wonder!

Miracle is often used in reference to an event that defies logical explanation and appears to be the work of a higher power, suggesting a reality beyond the five senses.

Here are some perspectives on identifying a miracle.

❶ Disregard most minor situations.
The facts should indicate a situation of high order, such as one that is life threatening, one involving suffering, or involving an immediate threat. Finding your lost keys does not necessarily constitute a miracle.

❷ Look for a lack of predictability.
A positive outcome should be needed and wanted, but not expected. Miracles tend to occur "out of the blue" rather than as the result of an earthly cause, especially a human one.

❸ Evaluate the outcome.
Miracles achieve a life-giving purpose; they never occur outside the will of God. Suffering is relieved, God is glorified, Jesus' presence is made manifest, the lowly are lifted up, evil is thwarted, creation is revealed, or life is saved. The outcome *must* be regarded as good, according to biblical standards.

④ Look for a divine agency.
The ability to make a miracle happen, to guarantee the results, or to take credit for it is beyond human capability. Often, the event will defy what we know to be true about the laws of nature or probability. If anyone stands to make money or advance an agenda from an event, it is most likely not a miracle.

⑤ Adopt a wait-and-see perspective.
A miracle will still be a miracle later on. Labeling something a miracle too quickly could lead down unhelpful paths. While waiting to make the call, pondering the event in your heart will enhance your faith journey.

Be Aware

- We should recognize God's work in both the extraordinary and ordinary events of life—and give God praise!
- We should "listen to our lives" to see ways in which we perceive God's work to be producing "wonder" in us!
- The greatest miracle of all is God's sending Jesus Christ into the world to give us "life" and "light" (John 1:4)!

THREE ESSENTIAL PERSONAL SPIRITUAL PRACTICES

A spiritual practice is a routine for building one's faith. Practice involves action, words, and often images that work together to center one's daily life in Jesus Christ. Medical studies show that people who pray regularly throughout the day suffer less stress, have lower incidence of heart disease, and live longer on average than those who do not.

❶ Morning Devotions
- Directly upon awakening, turn your attention first to God. The silence and solitude available in the morning hours are ideal.
- Try to make prayer the first activity of your day. If necessary, set your alarm to sound 15 minutes early to give yourself time.
- Begin with thanks and by remembering God's constant presence.
- Identify events you anticipate in your day and how you feel about them.
- Ask God to provide what you need for the day.
- Pray on behalf of other people. Consider keeping a list of names tucked inside your Bible or devotional book.

❷ Mealtime Grace
Human beings naturally pause before a meal. Use those moments to give thanks.
- Consider establishing mealtime grace as a household practice.

- When eating in public, be considerate of others, but do not abandon your practice.
- Once your meal is assembled and ready to eat, take time before praying to gather your thoughts and call an appropriate prayer to mind.
- Many people pray a rote or memorized prayer at mealtimes. Consider occasionally departing from your regular prayer with an extemporaneous one.

Praying before mealtime is a great personal practice that can be shared with others.

❸ Evening Prayer

The other daily practices you perform in the evening, like brushing your teeth or letting the cat out, create a natural structure for evening prayer.

- Establish a regular time, such as sunset or at bedtime, and commit to it.
- Confess wrongdoing and ask for forgiveness.
- Tell God about the joys and sorrows of the day. Ask for help with the sorrows and give thanks for the joys.
- Identify the good things about the day. On bad days, find at least one thing for which to give thanks.
- Consider using a devotional as a guide and companion.
- Think about involving other members of your household in this practice. Evening prayer particularly can be enhanced through sharing.

HOW TO FORGIVE SOMEONE

Forgiving is one of the most difficult disciplines of faith since it seems to cost you something additional when you've already been wronged. Swallowing your pride and seeking a greater good, however, can yield great healing and growth.

❶ Acknowledge that God forgives you.
When you realize that God has already shown forgiveness, and continues to forgive sinners like you, it's easier to forgive someone else.

❷ Consult Scripture.
Jesus taught the Lord's Prayer to his disciples, who were hungry to become like he was. Forgiveness was a big part of this. Read Matthew 6:9–15.

❸ Seek the person out whenever possible.
Consciously decide to deliver your forgiveness in person. In cases where this is geographically impossible, find an appropriate alternative means, such as the telephone.

Note: This may not be wise in all cases, given the timing of the situation or the level of hurt. Certain problems can be made worse by an unwelcome declaration of forgiveness. Consult with a clergyperson before taking questionable action.

❹ Say, "I forgive you," out loud.
A verbal declaration of forgiveness is ideal. Speaking the words enacts a physical chain reaction that can create healing for both speaker and hearer. In the Bible, Jesus used these words to heal a paralyzed man from across a room.

❺ Pray for the power to forgive.
Praying for this is always good, whether a forgiveness situation is at hand or not. It is especially helpful in cases where declaring forgiveness seems beyond your reach.

Be Aware

- When someone sins against you personally, forgiving them does NOT depend upon them feeling sorry (showing contrition) or asking for your forgiveness. But it helps. You may have to struggle, however, to forgive them without their consent or participation.

- When continual, hurting activities occur as cruel mistreatment, this is abuse. There is a need for help in these situations from a pastor or professional counselor. Those who are abused should take steps to deal with the situation where abuse occurs. They should seek the assistance of others who can assess the situation and intervene as needed. Forgiveness is no substitute for obtaining this type of help.

HOW TO CARE FOR THE SICK

While a trained and licensed physician must be sought to treat illness and injury, there is no malady that cannot be helped with faithful attention and prayer.

❶ Assess the nature of the problem.
Visit a local pharmacy if the illness is a simple one. Over-the-counter medications usually provide temporary relief until the body heals itself. If symptoms persist, the sick person should see a doctor and get a more detailed diagnosis.

❷ Pray for them.
Intercessory prayers are prayers made on someone else's behalf. Consider keeping a list of people who are sick so that you can remember them as you pray each day. Add the afflicted person to your church's prayer list.

❸ Call in the elders.
Prayer and emotional support from friends and family are vital parts of healing, living with illness, and facing death. Ask the pastor to assemble the church elders (leaders) for prayer and the laying on of hands.

Here's what the Bible says on this topic: "Are any among you sick? They should call for the elders of the church and have them pray over them, anointing them with oil in the name of the Lord" (James 5:14).

Be Aware

- Many people claim expertise in healing, from acupuncturists and herbalists to "faith healers" and psychics. Use caution and skepticism, but keep an open mind.

- Many people believe that much healing can be found in "comfort foods," such as homemade chicken soup. While the soup may or may not have healing properties, the loving care that a gift of soup represents most certainly does.
- Those who attempt to diagnose and treat their own symptoms can often do more harm than good. When in doubt, always consult a pharmacist, doctor, or other medical professional.

Gather friends, family, and church leaders to pray and lay hands on sick people.

Everyday Stuff

HOW TO IDENTIFY AND DEAL WITH EVIL

Christians are very aware of evil. We live in a world where evil is present. Most often, the Bible deals with evil as sin or what we can call moral evil. Evil emerges out of human choices to oppose God—to break God's laws; to focus on one's own desires instead of God's will; to harm others to get what we want. Evil results when sin reigns. Evil is the expression of the sin that rebels against God.

❶ Identifying Evil

- **Evil opposes the will of God.**

    When you encounter something that leads you away from what God wants: Watch out! It may be evil!

- **Evil exists in the human heart.**

    As sinful people, we all participate in evil.

- **Evil comes in many forms.**

    Some are very clear—hatred, killings, destruction.

    Some are very subtle and hard to detect—lies, deception, gossip.

- **Evil exists in groups of people and in societies and cultures.**

    Institutions that appear to do "good" may also participate in evil practices—discrimination, racism, sexism, ageism.

❷ Dealing with Evil

- Examine your life and **ask God to help you** identify attitudes, practices, and choices that oppose God.

Recognize that sin and evil reside within all of us and **ask for God's forgiveness.**

- **Actively work to eliminate** the evil that you find in your life.

- **Examine the groups in which you participate** to see what attitudes, practices, and choices they make and whether these are consistent with the will of God.

- **Work to eliminate evil practices** in the groups in which you participate.

- **Ask God to help you avoid evil and be a faithful Christian.**

Be Aware
- Evil practices may be pleasurable, even fun, making them difficult to identify or resist. Conversely, right practices and choices that glorify God may be difficult, even painful. Who says Christian discipleship is not an adventure!

HOW TO AVOID GOSSIP

Gossip is among the most corrosive forces within a community and should be monitored closely. Discovery of gossip should be viewed as an opportunity to defend your neighbors' integrity, both gossiper and gossipee.

1. Determine whether the conversation at hand qualifies as gossip.
   - Gossip involves one party speaking about a second party to a third party.
   - The person who is the topic of gossip is not a participant in the conversation.
   - The tone of the conversation is often secretive or negative. Gasps and whispers are common.
   - The facts expressed in a gossip conversation are often unsubstantiated and have been obtained second- or third-hand.

2. Recall and heed Titus 3:2: "Speak evil of no one."

3. Interject yourself into the conversation politely. Ask whether the gossipers have spoken directly to the person about whom they are talking. If not, politely ask why. This may give some indication why they are gossiping.

4. Make a statement of fact.
   Gossip withers in the face of truth. Make an attempt to parse out what is truly known from conjecture and supposition. State aloud that gossip is disrespectful and unfair.

Avoid gossip. It undermines community and damages relationships.

❺ Offer an alternative explanation based on fact. Describe other situations that cast the gossipee in a favorable light. Always try to give people the benefit of the doubt.

Be Aware

- There is a fine line between helping and meddling. Pay close attention to your own motivations and the possible outcomes of your actions.
- Gossip injures both the gossiper and the person who is the subject of rumors.
- Consult Exodus 20:16 and James 4:11.

Everyday Stuff

HOW TO RESOLVE INTERPERSONAL CONFLICT

Disagreements are part of life. They often occur when we forget that not everyone sees things the same way. Conflict should be viewed as an opportunity to grow, not a contest for domination.

❶ Adopt a healthy attitude.
Your frame of mind is critical. Approach the situation with forethought and calm. Prayer can be invaluable at this stage. Do not approach the other party when you're angry or upset.

❷ Read Matthew 18:15–20 beforehand.
Consult the Bible to orient your thinking. This is the model Jesus provided and can be used to call to mind an appropriate method.

❸ Talk directly to the person involved.
Avoid "triangulation." Talking about someone to a third party can make the conflict worse, as the person may feel that he or she is the subject of gossip. Speaking with the other person directly eliminates the danger and boosts the odds of a good outcome.

❹ Express yourself without attacking.
Using "I statements" can avoid casting the other person as the "bad guy" and inflaming the conflict. "I statements" are sentences beginning with phrases such as "I feel . . . " or "I'm uncomfortable when . . ."

5 Keep "speaking the truth in love" (Ephesians 4:15) as your goal.
Your "truth" may not be the same as that of the other party. Your objective is to discover and honor each other's "truth," not to put down the other person. Be ready to admit your own faults and mistakes.

6 Seek out a third party to act as an impartial witness.
If direct conversation doesn't resolve the conflict, locate someone both parties trust to sit in. This can help clarify your positions and bring understanding.

7 Build toward forgiveness and a renewed friendship.
Agree upon how you will communicate to prevent future misunderstandings.

Be Aware

- Seemingly unrelated events in your or the other person's life may be playing an invisible role in the conflict at hand. Be ready to shift the focus to the real cause.

- You may not be able to resolve the conflict at this time, but don't give up on future opportunities.

When two people aren't getting along, sometimes an impartial third person can help resolve the dispute.

Everyday Stuff

HOW TO CONSOLE SOMEONE

Consolation is a gift from God. Christians in turn give it to others to build up the body of Christ and preserve it in times of trouble. (See 2 Corinthians 1:4–7.) Cumberland Presbyterians often employ food as a helpful secondary means.

1. **Listen first.**
   Make it known that you're present and available. When the person opens up, be quiet and attentive.

2. **Be ready to help the person face grief and sadness, not avoid them.**
   The object is to help the person name, understand, and work through feelings, not gloss over them.

3. **Avoid saying things to make yourself feel better.**
   "I know exactly how you feel," is seldom true and trivializes the sufferer's pain. Even if you have experienced something similar, no experience is exactly the same. If there is nothing to say, simply be present with the person.

4. **Show respect with honesty.**
   Don't try to answer the mysteries of the universe or force your beliefs on the person. Be clear about your limitations. Be ready to let some questions go unanswered. Consolation isn't about having all the answers, it's about bearing one another's burdens.

5. **Don't put words in God's mouth.**
   Avoid saying, "This is God's will," or, "This is part of God's plan." Unless you heard it straight from God, don't say it.

HOW TO COPE WITH LOSS AND GRIEF

Cumberland Presbyterians tend to downplay their losses by saying, "Well, it could be worse." This may provide only temporary relief at best. Any loss can cause pain, feelings of confusion, and uncertainty. These responses are normal.

① Familiarize yourself with the dimensions of grief.
Experts identify five: denial, anger, bargaining, depression, and acceptance. Some add hope as a sixth dimension. These occur in no particular order and grieving persons may bounce around among them, sometimes experiencing two or three in a single day. This is normal.

② Express your grief.
Healthy ways may include crying, staring into space for extended periods, ruminating, shouting at the ceiling, and sudden napping. Laughing outbursts are also appropriate and should not be judged harshly.

③ Identify someone you trust with whom you can talk.
Available people can include a spouse, parents, relatives, friends, a pastor, a doctor, or a trained counselor. Many household pets also make good listeners and willing confidants.

④ Choose a personal way to memorialize the loss.
Make a collage of photographs, offer a memorial donation to your church, or start a scrapbook of memories to honor the event. This helps you to begin to heal without getting stuck in your grief.

Be Aware

- Many experts prescribe a self-giving activity, such as volunteering at a shelter or soup kitchen, as a means of facilitating a healthy grieving process.
- The pain immediately after suffering a loss is usually deep and intense. This will lessen with the passage of time, though it may never go away completely. Many people experience—and may be unsettled by—sudden bursts of grief even years and decades following a loss.
- Short-term depression may occur in extreme cases. After experiencing a great loss, such as the death of a loved one, make an appointment with your family physician for a physical.
- Even Jesus cried when his friend Lazarus died (John 11:35).

Even Jesus felt the loss of Lazarus when he died.

Mary   Martha

THE TOP TEN ATTRIBUTES TO LOOK FOR IN A SPOUSE

While no single personality trait can predict a compatible marriage, the following list frames the basic things to look for in a spouse. With all attributes, some differences can be the source of a couple's strength rather than a source of difficulty. Statistically, Cumberland Presbyterians appear to be about as successful at choosing a spouse as other people.

❶ Similar values.
Values that concern religious beliefs, life purpose, financial priorities, and children are a foundation on which to build the relationship. Contrary values tend to create discord.

❷ Physical-energy and physical-space compatibility.
Consider whether the person's energy level and physical space needs work with yours. Also, the word *compatibility* can mean a complementary match of opposites, or it can denote a match based on strong similarities.

❸ Physical and romantic compatibility.
If the two of you have a similar degree of interest in or need for physical and romantic expression in your relationship, the chance of lifelong compatibility increases.

❹ Intellectual parity.
Communicating with someone who has a significantly different intelligence level or educational background can require extra effort.

Everyday Stuff

❺ Emotional maturity.
A lifelong relationship of mutual challenge and support often helps each person grow emotionally, but a lifetime spent waiting for someone to grow up could be more frustration than it's worth.

❻ Sense of humor.
A sense of humor can provide an excellent measure of a person's personality and an important means to couple survival. If he or she doesn't get your jokes, you could be asking for trouble.

❼ Respect.
Look for someone who listens to you without trying to control you. Look also for a healthy sense of self-respect.

❽ Trustworthiness.
Seek out someone who is honest and acts with your best interests in mind—not only his or hers—and tries to learn from his or her mistakes.

❾ Forgiving.
When you sincerely apologize to your spouse, he or she should try to work through and get beyond the problem rather than hold on to it. Once forgiven, past mistakes should not be raised, especially in conflict situations.

❿ Kindness.
An attitude of consistent kindness may be the most critical attribute for a lifelong partnership.

Be Aware
- If you live to be old, you will probably experience major changes that you cannot predict at age 15 or 25 or 35. Accepting this fact in advance can help you weather difficult times.
- Use all of your resources—intuition, emotions, and rational thought—to make the decision about a life partner.
- Family members and trusted friends can offer invaluable advice in this decision-making process and should be consulted.

HOW TO BE SAVED (BY GRACE THROUGH FAITH AND NOT BY YOUR GOOD WORKS)

Many religions are built on the idea that the more closely people follow the religious rules or the more morally people behave, the better God will like them—and the better God likes them, the greater their chances of "getting into heaven."

While there is nothing wrong with moral living or obeying God's laws, that kind of behavior has very little to do with the salvation God offers. Even people who are not followers of Jesus Christ may live moral lives.

Christianity, on the other hand, says that out of pure love God was willing to sacrifice everything—even God's only Son—to save you forever from sin, death, and all your false gods. Including you.

Since God has already done everything needed to secure your salvation through Jesus, you never have to do one single thing to earn God's favor, no matter how bad you are at following the rules. Still, being saved takes some getting used to.

❶ Get familiar with the word *grace*.
Grace means that God gives you all the good stuff—forgiveness, salvation, love, and life, with all its ups and downs—as totally free gifts. Keep an eye out for situations in which you can use this word, and then use it liberally. You'll soon begin to see God's grace all around you.

❷ Practice letting go of things you love.
Staying focused on yourself can make it difficult to open up to a grace-filled world. But giving of yourself, your time, and your possessions can put you in a receptive, open frame of mind. This is important, as salvation cannot be "found" by looking for it; it is only revealed.

❸ Lose yourself as often as possible.
An important part of having a receptive frame of mind is losing yourself in whatever you're doing. To do this, give yourself over entirely to the activity. This can be accomplished in prayer and worship, but also through things like playing games, talking with friends and family, reading a good book, serving others, or playing a musical instrument. Even work can accomplish this.

❹ Admit your limitations.
Without straying into despair or false modesty, make an honest confession to yourself about what you can and cannot do, what you are and what you are not. When you see yourself realistically you become more open to God's message of love, grace, and salvation.

❺ Accept your uniqueness.
You are created in the image of God. You are specially "you." Like snowflakes, every person is unique. Accept your uniqueness. God loves you in your specialness, your you-ness. God can use you to do things God wants done in the world. So treasure your gifts and enjoy being you.

❻ Spend time in worship and prayer to the living God.
While only God grants the faith that saves, the church gives lots of opportunities where God has promised to come to you.

7 Avoid the temptation to "do."
The "old Adam" or "old Eve" in you—the sinner in you—always wants to be in charge over God. He or she will tell you that God's grace is too good to be true and that you must "do" something to earn or justify it. Simply remind him or her that you were baptized into Jesus Christ and have all the grace you need.

Be Aware
- The apostle Paul's summary of the gospel goes like this: "For by grace you have been saved through faith, and this is not your own doing; it is the gift of God—not the result of works, so that no one may boast" (Ephesians 2:8–9).
- This viewpoint about God's grace, even among many Christians, is unpopular, as it was when the Reformers reminded the church of it almost 500 years ago. Be aware that once you adopt it you will come under fire and be tempted to lapse back into the old way.

GRACE

Getting familiar with this very important word will help you get used to being saved.

HOW TO UNDERSTAND THE TRINITY AS ONE GOD IN THREE PERSONS

The Trinity is a mystery. Even the great theologians don't completely understand how God can be "one God in three persons." Some scholars spend their whole lives studying it. After two thousand years, Christians still believe in this mystery because it gives life and shape to everything in our lives: our relationships, our faith, and especially our worship.

Here is an ancient symbol of the Trinity.

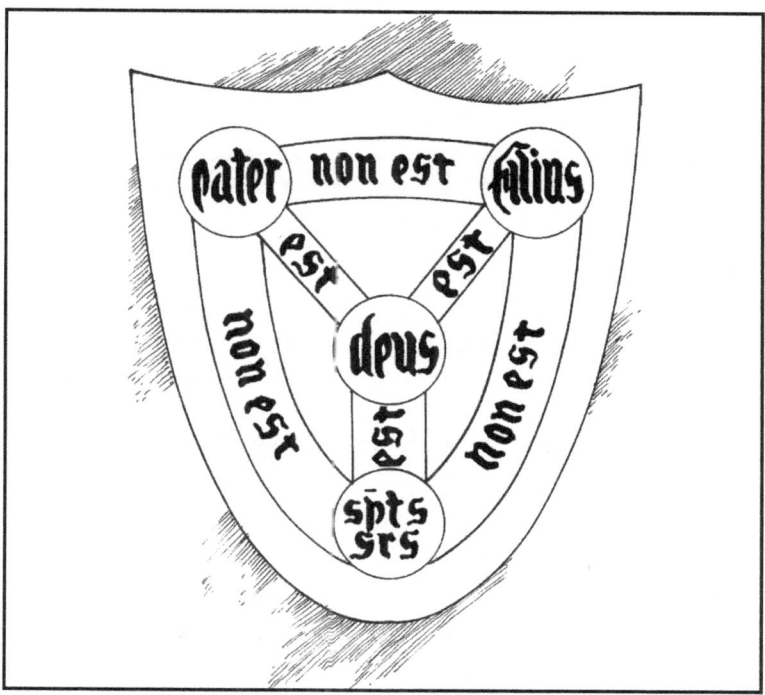

Everyday Stuff

The Trinity affirms:

- God is Father, Son, and Holy Spirit.
- The Father is not the Son.
- The Spirit is not the Son.
- The Father is not the Spirit.
- The Father is God.
- The Son is God.
- The Spirit is God.

The great mystery of the Trinity has many important implications for living the Christian life.

❶ God is not "three-faced."
All of God participates in all God's activities. We will not find opposition among the persons of the Trinity. So, what we believe the Holy Spirit is leading us toward in our lives will not be contrary to what God the Father has revealed or God the Son has shown us. We can have confidence in God as Father, Son, and Holy Spirit.

❷ Divine and Human Community.
The three persons of the Trinity share the "divine community," whose bond is love. The Trinity provides a model for the human community, since humans are created in the image of God and find their fullest life by living in a community of fellowship with others and with God. We will not seek isolated lives, but communal lives.

❸ A Model for Love.
"God is love" (1 John 4:16) and God's people are to share love with one other because "love is from God" (1 John

4:7). Love is shared among the three persons of the Trinity, and those who love God will share love in the human community and in all our relationships. We live love with one another.

HOW TO TALK TO FRIENDS ABOUT THE CUMBERLAND PRESBYTERIAN CHURCH

Every Christian denomination is unique. But you know that or you wouldn't be reading this book. Sometimes people who do not know the Cumberland Presbyterian Church will ask questions about our quirks and eccentricities. Here are some of the most frequently asked questions and some ideas for answering them.

What's the difference between Cumberland Presbyterians and "regular" Presbyterians?

The short answer today is "not that much." But at the time the Cumberland Presbyterian Church was formed in 1810 it differed theologically from its mother church on the doctrine of predestination (which the early Cumberland Presbyterians rejected as "fatalism"), the question of whether or not God saved infants who died (the Cumberland Presbyterians believed God does), and a few other issues. The upstart Cumberland Presbyterians also differed with the Presbyterian Church about the ways ministers needed to be educated in order to preach the Gospel on the frontiers of America that were opening up in the early 19th century. Cumberland Presbyterians wanted to establish schools near the frontier to educate ministers. The Presbyterian Church required ministers to obtain a classical education at schools in the northeast. In 1903 the Presbyterian Church moderated its theological statement on predestination, which paved the way in 1906 for a partial reuniting of the Cumberland Presbyterian Church with the mother church. About a third of Cumberland Presbyterians declined to go with the union and continued the denomination. Today, Presbyterians and Cumberland Presbyterians enjoy warm relations and cooperate on a number of joint ministries.

How did the Cumberland Presbyterian Church get started?
The people who began the church were Presbyterians who were influenced by the Great Revival that sprang up in America in the late 1700s and early 1800s. They experienced God the Holy Spirit through Word and Sacrament and wanted to push west to share the Good News about Jesus Christ with others who lived on the frontier. This led to the afore-mentioned theological and ecclesiastical conflicts within the Presbyterian Church. On February 4, 1810, near Dickson, Tennessee, three ministers, Finis Ewing, Samuel McAdow, and Samuel King constituted Cumberland Presbytery. In time they grew and into three presbyteries and formed Cumberland Synod (1813). The church expanded rapidly and formed a General Assembly in 1829.

Why are there two Cumberland Presbyterian denominations?
There are two Cumberland Presbyterian denominations because, following the Civil War, the Cumberland Presbyterians who had been freed from slavery began a separate church. In part this happened because African American members wanted to express ecclesiastically the freedoms they were experiencing in society as a whole. But it's more complicated than that. The racism of the time and the failures of the white Cumberland Presbyterians to support African American efforts were also contributing factors. On May 1, 1874, the General Assembly of the Cumberland Presbyterian Church, Colored was constituted in Nashville, Tennessee. Now called the Cumberland Presbyterian Church in America, the denomination has been an important

Everyday Stuff 117

witness to Christ through the African American experience. Today the two Cumberland Presbyterian denomina- tions work together closely on historical preservation, youth ministry programs and many other discipleship ministries. The churches share a common Confession of Faith, written as a cooperative effort and adopted by both churches in 1984. The headquarters for the Cumberland Presbyterian Church in America is in Huntsville, Alabama; the Cumberland Presbyterian Center is in Memphis, Tennessee.

Is the Cumberland Presbyterian Church a Bible-based Church?
Yes. Every statement in our Confession of Faith is based on insights gained from scripture. We believe that God the Holy Spirit speaks through scripture to enlighten and sustain the Church and individual Christians. We affirm that the scriptures are "the infallible rule of faith and practice, the authoritative guide for Christian living." This means that people who rely on scripture to live their faith can live confidently. Be careful though! "Bible-based" is sometimes code language for reading Scripture literally. The Cumberland Presbyterian Church has never taught a literal interpretation of the Bible. We believe that interpreting Scripture is the work of God the Holy Spirit in conjunction with our prayerful study of the writings, their historical contexts, and the teaching of the church through the centuries.

Are Cumberland Presbyterians liberal or conservative?
Yes. And everything in between. Mostly in between.

Is the Cumberland Presbyterian Church multi-ethnic?
Yes. Our church includes people from a wide variety of racial-ethnic backgrounds and nationalities. In the United States Cumberland Presbyterians worship in such languages

as English, Choctaw, Spanish, Chinese, and Korean. New congregations have been established among Korean and Sudanese immigrants in recent years. Outside the United States, congregations can be found in Japan, Korea, Laos, Hong Kong, Colombia, and Brazil.

How do Cumberland Presbyterians relate to other Christian bodies?

Cumberland Presbyterians have a long tradition of working with Christians across denominational lines. We hold membership in the World Alliance of Reformed Churches, headquartered in Geneva, Switzerland. We have worked closely with others in publishing educational materials. We pursue a variety of mission and relief efforts through cooperation with other denominations.

Does the Cumberland Presbyterian Church have any schools?

From the very beginning, Cumberland Presbyterians established colleges and universities. At the time of the partial reunion with the Presbyterian Church in 1906, we had more than twenty institutions of higher learning. Almost all of those went into the union. Currently we support Bethel University in McKenzie, Tennessee, a private liberal arts school. Memphis Theological Seminary in Memphis, Tennessee, is owned by the church and prepares women and men for ministry in the Cumberland Presbyterian Church and more than twenty-five other denominations.

BIBLE STUFF

Written down by many people over hundreds of years, the Bible is more like a portable bookshelf than one book by itself. And because the Bible is God's Word, people often feel overwhelmed when they try to read it.

This section includes:

- Helpful information about when, where, and why people wrote the 66 books within the Bible. (It didn't all come together at once.)
- Tips for reading and understanding the Bible—how it's organized and what it says.
- Some of the most mystifying, hair-raising, and just plain off-the-wall stories in the Bible.

COMMON TRANSLATIONS OF THE BIBLE

Translation	Grade Level*	Theological Affiliation	Year Released	Special Features
King James Version	12.0	Church of England, conservative and evangelical	1611	Poetic style using Elizabethan English. Most widely used translation for centuries.
New American Standard Bible	11.0	Conservative and evangelical	1971; updated, 1995	Revision of the 1901 American Standard Version into contemporary language.
New Revised Standard Version	8.1	Mainline and interconfessional	1989	Updated version of the Revised Standard Version.
New King James Version	8.0	Transnational, transdenominational, conservative, and evangelical	1982	Updates the King James text into contemporary language.
New International Version	7.8	Transnational, transdenominational, conservative, and evangelical	1978; revised, 1984	Popular modern-language version. Attempts to balance literal and dynamic translation methods.
Today's English Version (also called the Good News Bible)	7.3	Evangelical and interconfessional	1976	Noted for its freshness of language.

New American Bible	6.6	Roman Catholic	1970; revised NT, 1986; revised Psalms, 1991	Official translation of the Roman Catholic Church in the United States.
New Living Translation	6.4	Evangelical	1996	A meaning-for-meaning translation. Successor to the Living Bible.
New Century Version	5.6	Conservative and evangelical	1988; revised, 1991	Follows the *Living Word Vocabulary*.
Contemporary English Version	5.4	Conservative, evangelical, mainline	1995	Easy-to-read English for new Bible readers.
The Message	4.8, from NT samples	Evangelical	2002	An expressive paraphrase of the Bible.

*The grade level on which the text is written, using Dale-chall, Fry, Raygor, and Spache Formulas.

Bible classifications

Apocrypha Bible: Contains certain books that Protestants don't consider canonical. Most of these OT books are accepted by the Roman Catholic Church.

Children's Bible: Includes illustrations and other study aids that are especially helpful for children.

Concordance Bible: Lists places in the Bible where key words are found.

Red Letter Bible: The words spoken by Christ appear in red.

Reference Bible: Pages include references to other Bible passages on the same subject.

Self-Proclaiming Bible: Diacritical marks (as in a dictionary) appear above difficult names and words to help with the pronunciation.

Text Bible: Contains text without footnotes or column references. May include maps, illustrations, and other helpful material.

Bible Stuff

60 ESSENTIAL BIBLE STORIES

	Story	Bible Text	Key Verse
1.	Creation	Genesis 1–2	Genesis 1:27
2.	The Human Condition	Genesis 3–4	Genesis 3:5
3.	The Flood and the First Covenant	Genesis 6–9	Genesis 9:8
4.	The Tower of Babel and Abraham and Sarah	Genesis 11–12	Genesis 12:1
5.	Sarah, Hagar, and Abraham	Genesis 12–25	Genesis 17:19
6.	Isaac and Rebecca	Genesis 22–25	Genesis 24:67
7.	Jacob and Esau	Genesis 25–36	Genesis 28:15
8.	Joseph and God's Hidden Ways	Genesis 37–50	Genesis 50:20
9.	Moses and Pharaoh	Exodus 1–15	Exodus 2:23
10.	The Ten Commandments	Exodus 20	Exodus 20:2
11.	From the Wilderness into the Promised Land	Exodus 16–18; Deuteronomy 1–6; Joshua 1–3, 24	Deuteronomy 6:4
12.	Judges	Book of Judges	Judges 21:25
13.	Ruth	Book of Ruth	Ruth 4:14
14.	Samuel and Saul	1 Samuel 1–11	1 Samuel 3:1
15.	King David	multiple OT books	1 Samuel 8:6
16.	David, Nathan, and What Is a Prophet?	2 Samuel 11–12	2 Samuel 7:12
17.	Solomon	1 Kings 1–11	1 Kings 6:12
18.	Split of the Kingdom	1 Kings 11ff	1 Kings 12:16
19.	Northern Kingdom, Its Prophets and Fate	1 Kings–2 Kings 17	Amos 5:21
20.	Southern Kingdom, Its Prophets and Fate (Part 1)	multiple OT books	Isaiah 5:7

60 ESSENTIAL BIBLE STORIES

	Story	Bible Text	Key Verse
21.	Southern Kingdom, Its Prophets and Fate (Part 2)	multiple OT books	Jeremiah 31:31
22.	The Exile	Isaiah 40–55; Ezekiel	Isaiah 40:10
23.	Return from Exile	multiple OT books	Ezra 1:1
24.	Ezra and Nehemiah	Books of Ezra and Nehemiah	Ezra 3:10
25.	Esther	Book of Esther	Esther 4:14
26.	Job	Book of Job	Job 1:1
27.	Daniel	Book of Daniel	Daniel 3:17
28.	Psalms of Praise and Trust	Psalms 8, 30, 100, 113, 121	Psalm 121:1
29.	Psalms for Help	various psalms	Psalm 22:1
30.	Wisdom	Job, Proverbs, Ecclesiastes	Proverbs 1:7
31.	The Annunciation	Luke 1:26–56	Luke 1:31–33
32.	Magi	Matthew 2:1–12	Matthew 2:2–3
33.	Birth of Jesus	Luke 2:1–20	Luke 2:10–11
34.	Simeon	Luke 2:25–35	Luke 2:30–32
35.	Wilderness Temptations	Matthew 4:1–11; Mark 1:12–13; Luke 4:1–13	Luke 4:12–13
36.	Jesus' Nazareth Sermon	Matthew 13:54–58; Mark 6:1–6: Luke 4:16–30	Luke 4:18–19, 21
37.	Jesus Calls the First Disciples	Matthew 4:18–22; Mark 1:16–20; Luke 5:1–11	Luke 5:9–10
38.	Beatitudes	Matthew 5:3–12	Luke 6:20–26
39.	Gerasene Demoniac	Matthew 8:28–34; Mark 5:1–20; Luke 8:26–39	Luke 8:39
40.	Feeding of the 5,000	Matthew 14:13–21; Mark 6:30–44; Luke 9:10–17; John 6:1–14	Luke 9:16–17

Bible Stuff

60 ESSENTIAL BIBLE STORIES

	Story	Bible Text	Key Verse
41.	The Transfiguration	Matthew 17:1–8; Mark 9:2–8: Luke 9:28–36	Luke 9:34–35
42.	Sending of the Seventy	Matthew 8:19–22; Luke 10:1–16	Luke 10:8, 16
43.	Good Samaritan	Luke 10:25–37	Luke 10:27–28
44.	Healing the Bent-Over Woman	Luke 13:10–17	Luke 13:16
45.	Parables of Lost and Found	Luke 15:1–32	Luke 15:31–32
46.	Rich Man and Lazarus	Luke 16:19–31	Luke 16:29–31
47.	Zacchaeus	Luke 19:1–11	Luke 19:9
48.	Sheep and Goats	Matthew 25:31–46	Matthew 25:40
49.	Parable of the Vineyard	Matthew 21:33–46; Mark 12:1–12; Luke 20:9–19; (Isaiah 5:1–7)	Luke 20:14–16
50.	The Last Supper	Matthew 26:20–29; Mark 14:12–16: Luke 22:14–38	Luke 22:19–20, 27
51.	Crucifixion	Matthew 27; Mark 15; Luke 23; John 19	Luke 23:42–43, 46
52.	Road to Emmaus	Luke 24	Luke 24:30–31
53.	Pentecost	Acts 2:1–21	Acts 2:17–18
54.	Healing the Lame Man	Acts 3–4	Acts 4:19
55.	Baptism of the Ethiopian	Acts 8:26–39	Acts 8:35–37
56.	Call of Saul	Acts 7:58–8:1, 9:1–30	Acts 9:15–16
57.	Peter and Cornelius	Acts 10	Acts 10:34–35
58.	Philippians' Humility	Philippians 2:1–13	Philippians 2:12–13
59.	Love Hymn	1 Corinthians 13	1 Corinthians 13:4–7
60.	Resurrection	1 Corinthians 15	1 Corinthians 15:51–55

HOW TO READ THE BIBLE

The Bible is a collection of 66 separate books gathered together over hundreds of years and thousands of miles. Divided into the Old Testament (Hebrew language) and the New Testament (Greek language), these writings have many authors and take many forms.

The Bible includes histories, stories, prophecies, poetry, songs, teachings, and laws, to name a few. Christians believe the Bible is the story of God's relationship with humankind and a powerful way that God speaks to people.

❶ Determine your purpose for reading.

Clarify in your own mind what you hope to gain. Your motivations should be well intentioned, such as to seek information, to gain a deeper understanding of God and yourself, or to enrich your faith. Pray for insight before every reading time.

❷ Resolve to read daily.

Commit to a daily regimen of Bible reading. Make it a part of your routine until it becomes an unbreakable habit.

Commit to reading the Bible daily.

❸ Master the mechanics.
- Memorize the books of the Bible in order.
- Familiarize yourself with the introductory material. Many Bible translations include helpful information at the front of the Bible and at the beginning of each book.

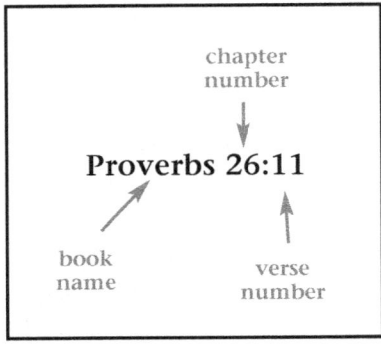

- The books are broken down into chapters and verses. Locate the beginning of a book by using the Bible's table of contents. Follow the numerical chapter numbers; these are usually in large type. Verses are likewise numbered in order within each chapter. Simply run your finger down the page until you locate the verse number you're looking for.
- If your Bible contains maps (usually in the back), consult them when cities, mountains, or seas are mentioned in your reading.

❹ Befriend the written text.
Read with a pen or pencil in hand and underline passages of interest. Look up unfamiliar words in a dictionary. Write notes in the margins when necessary. The Bible was written to be read and used, not worshiped.

❺ Practice reading from the Bible out loud.

HOW TO INTERPRET THE BIBLE

Interpreting the Bible is not an easy task. We recognize that the Bible is a library of ancient books, written over centuries of time, by people far different from us, and in cultures greatly different from our own. The Bible was written in languages we do not read: the Old Testament in Hebrew; the New Testament in Greek. So, we rely on English translations to provide our biblical texts.

Today we have many resources to help us interpret Scripture. We should make use of a variety of English translations of the Bible, biblical commentaries, and other aids to enable us to gain a good grasp on what the Bible is saying.

Cumberland Presbyterians recognize the importance of using the best resources of scholarship to help us in the important task of biblical interpretation.

Here are some tips for interpreting the Bible.

- Jesus Christ is the central focus of Scripture.

    The Bible proclaims the good news of God's love in Jesus Christ. This is the gospel message the church proclaims.

- We should interpret the plain text of Scripture in its grammatical, historical, and cultural contexts instead of seeking allegories or "hidden meanings."

    We should try to understand the words, setting, and type of writing of each biblical text. The Bible's message is open to all and we do not pursue hidden or adventurous approaches to interpretation.

Bible Stuff

- Our interpretation of the Bible requires use of reliable resources.

    We should use the best scholarly tools to help us interpret the settings and contexts in which God's divine message in Scripture has come to us.

- The Holy Spirit helps us to interpret and apply God's message.

    We should always pray for the Holy Spirit to help us hear God's Word when we read and study Scripture.

- Our interpretation of Scripture should accord with the rule of love.

    We should always ask whether our interpretation of Scripture is in accord with the twofold commandment Jesus gave: to love God and to love our neighbor (Matthew 22:34–40; Mark 12:28–34; Luke 10:25–28). People sometimes forget to do this.

HOW TO MEMORIZE A BIBLE VERSE

Memorizing Scripture is an ancient faith practice. Its value is often mentioned by people who have, in crisis situations, remembered comforting or reassuring passages coming to mind, sometimes decades after first memorizing them. There are three common methods of memorization.

Method 1: Memorize with Music

Choose a verse that is special for you. It is more difficult to remember something that doesn't make sense to you or that lacks meaning.

❶ Choose a familiar tune.
Pick something catchy and repetitious.

❷ Add the words from the Bible verse to your tune.
Mix up the words a bit, if necessary. Memorizing a verse "word for word" isn't always as important as learning the message of the verse.

❸ Mark the verse in your Bible.
This will help you find it again later on. Consider highlighting or underlining it.

❹ Make the words rhyme, if possible.

Method 2: The Three S's (See it, Say it, Script it)

This method works on the principle of multisensory reinforcement. The brain creates many more neural pathways to a memory through sight, speech, and manipulation (writing) than just one of these, so recall is quicker and easier.

❶ Write the verse on index cards in large print.
Post the cards in places you regularly look, such as the refrigerator door or bathroom mirror.

❷ Say the verse out loud.
Repeat the verse 10 times to yourself every time you notice one of your index cards.

❸ Write the verse down.

❹ Try saying and writing the verse at the same time. Repeat.

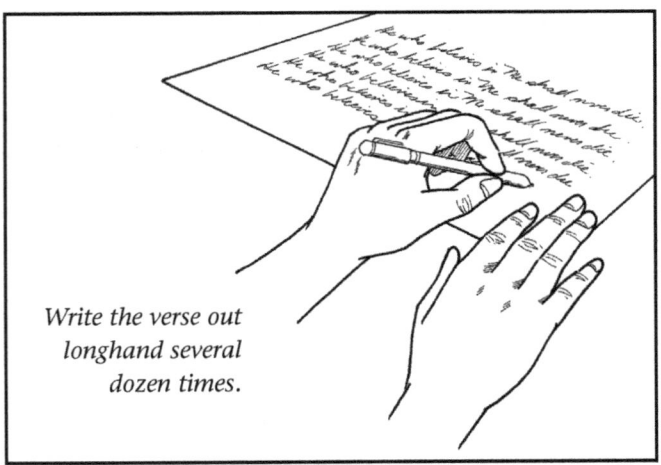

Write the verse out longhand several dozen times.

Method 3: Old-Fashioned Memorization
Attempt this method only if you consider yourself to be "old school" or if the other methods fail.

① Write the verse out by hand on paper.
A whiteboard can work extremely well, also. Consider writing it as many as 100 times. Repeat this process until you can recite the verse flawlessly.

② Don't get up until you've memorized the verse.
Open your Bible to the appropriate verse, sit down in front of it, and don't get up, eat, sleep, or use the bathroom until you can recite it flawlessly.

③ Enlist a family member or friend to help you.
Have them read along with you and prompt you when you get stuck.

TEN BIBLE VILLAINS

❶ Satan
The Evil One is known by many names in the Bible and appears many places, but the devil's purpose is always the same: To disrupt and confuse people so they turn from God and seek to become their own gods. This Bible villain is still active today.

❷ The Serpent
In Eden, the serpent succeeded in tempting Eve to eat from the tree of the knowledge of good and evil (Genesis 3:1–7). As a result, sin entered creation. If it not for the serpent, we'd all still be walking around naked, eating fresh fruit, and living forever.

❸ Pharaoh (probably Seti I or Rameses II)
The notorious Pharaoh from the book of Exodus enslaved the Israelites. Moses eventually begged him to "Let my people go," but Pharaoh hardened his heart and refused. Ten nasty plagues later, Pharaoh relented, but then changed his mind again. In the end, with his army at the bottom of the sea, Pharaoh finally gave his slaves up to the wilderness.

❹ Goliath
"The Philistine of Gath," who stood six cubits in height (about nine feet tall), was sent to fight David, still a wet-behind-the-ears youth of 15. Goliath was a fighting champion known for killing people, but David drilled Goliath in the head with a rock from his sling and gave God the glory (1 Samuel 17).

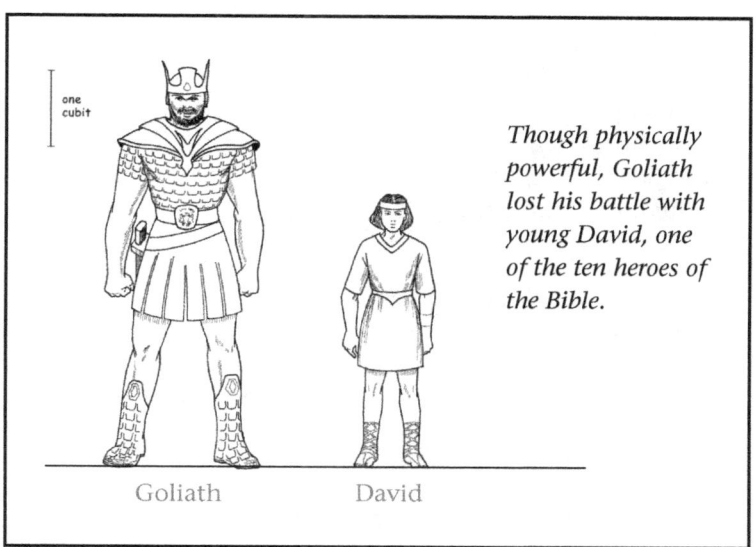

Though physically powerful, Goliath lost his battle with young David, one of the ten heroes of the Bible.

Goliath   David

❺ Jezebel

King Ahab of Judah's wife and a follower of the false god Baal, Jezebel led her husband away from God and tried to kill off the prophets of the Lord. Elijah the prophet, however, was on the scene. He shamed Jezebel's false prophets and killed them (1 Kings 18:40).

❻ King Herod

Afraid of any potential threat to his power, upon hearing about the birth of the Messiah in Bethlehem Herod sent the wise men to pinpoint his location. Having received a vision from God, the wise men went home by a different route and avoided Herod. In a rage, Herod ordered the murder of every child two years of age or younger in the vicinity of Bethlehem. The baby Messiah escaped with his parents to Egypt (Matthew 2:14–15).

⑦ The Pharisees, Sadducees, and Scribes
They dogged Jesus throughout his ministry, alternately challenging his authority and being awed by his power. It was their leadership, with the consent and blessing of the people and the Roman government that brought Jesus to trial and execution.

⑧ Judas
One of Jesus' original disciples, Judas earned 30 pieces of silver by betraying his Lord over to the authorities. He accomplished this by leading the soldiers into the garden of Gethsemane where he identified Jesus with a kiss (Matthew 26–27).

⑨ Pontius Pilate
The consummate politician, the Roman governor chose to preserve his own bloated status by giving the people what they wanted: Jesus' crucifixion. He washed his hands to signify self-absolution, but bloodied them instead.

⑩ God's People
They whine, they sin, they turn their backs on God over and over again. When given freedom, they blow it. When preached repentance by God's prophets, they stone them. When offered a Savior, we kill him. In the end, it must be admitted, God's people—us!—don't really shine. Only by God's grace and the gift of faith in Jesus Christ do we have hope.

TEN BIBLE HEROES

The Bible is filled with typical examples of heroism, but another kind of hero inhabits the pages of the Bible—those people who, against all odds, follow God no matter the outcome. These are heroes of faith.

❶ Noah

In the face of ridicule from others, Noah trusted God when God chose him to build an ark to save a remnant of humanity from destruction. Noah's trust became part of a covenant with God.

Noah trusted God, even though others made fun of him. By following God's instructions and building a great ark, Noah and his family survived the flood (Genesis 6–10).

❷ Abraham and Sarah
In extreme old age, Abraham and Sarah answered God's call to leave their home and travel to a strange land, where they became the parents of God's people.

❸ Moses
Moses, a man with a speech impediment, challenged the Egyptian powers to deliver God's people from bondage. He led a rebellious and contrary people for 40 years through the wilderness and gave them God's law.

❹ Rahab
A prostitute who helped Israel conquer the promised land, Rahab was the great-grandmother of King David, and thus a part of the family of Jesus himself.

❺ David
The youngest and smallest member of his family, David became king. He defeated great enemies, turning Israel into a world power. He wrote psalms, led armies, and confessed his sins to the Lord.

❻ Mary and Joseph
These humble peasants responded to God's call to be the parents of the Messiah, although the call came through a pregnancy that was not the result of marriage.

❼ The Canaanite Woman
Desperate for her daughter's health, the Canaanite woman challenged Jesus regarding women and race by claiming God's love for all people (Matthew 15:21–28). Because of this, Jesus praised her faith.

8 Peter
Peter was a man quick to speak but slow to think. At Jesus' trial, Peter denied ever having known him. But in the power of forgiveness and through Christ's appointment, Peter became a leader in the early church.

9 Saul/Paul
Originally an enemy and persecutor of Christians, Paul experienced a powerful vision of Jesus, converted, and became the greatest missionary the church has ever known.

10 Phoebe
A contemporary of Paul's, Phoebe is believed to have delivered the book of Romans after traveling some 800 miles from Cenchrea near Corinth to Rome. A wealthy woman, she used her influence to travel, protect other believers, and to host worship services in her home.

Phoebe is believed to have delivered the book of Romans after traveling 800 miles.

Bible Stuff

THE THREE MOST REBELLIOUS THINGS JESUS DID

❶ The prophet returned to his hometown (Luke 4:14–27). Jesus returned to Nazareth, where he was raised, and was invited to read Scripture and preach. First, he insisted that the Scriptures he read were not just comforting promises of a distant future, but that they were about him, local boy, anointed by God. Second, he insisted God would bless foreigners with those same promises through him. These statements amounted to the unpardonable crime of blasphemy!

❷ The rebel thumbed his nose at the authorities (John 11:55–12:11).
Jesus had become an outlaw, hunted by the religious authorities who wanted to kill him. Mary, Martha, and Lazarus threw a thank-you party for Jesus in Bethany, right outside Jerusalem, the authorities' stronghold. In spite of the threats to his life, Jesus went to the party. This was not just rebellion but a demonstration of how much Jesus loved his friends.

❸ The king rode a royal procession right under Caesar's nose (Matthew 21:1–17; Mark 11:1–10; Luke 19:28–38; John 12:12–19).
Jesus entered Jerusalem during a great festival, in full view of adoring crowds, as a king come home to rule. Riding the colt, heralded by the people with cloaks and branches, accompanied by the royal anthem (Psalm 118), he rode in to claim Jerusalem for God and himself as God's anointed. The Roman overlords and the Jewish leaders watched this seditious act and prepared for a crucifixion.

THE SEVEN FUNNIEST BIBLE STORIES

Humor isn't scarce in the Bible; you just have to look for it. For example, God tells Abraham (100 years old) and Sarah (in her 90s) they'll soon have a son. Understandably, they laugh. Later, they have a son named Isaac, which means "he laughs." Bible humor is also ironic, gross, and sometimes just plain bizarre.

❶ **Gideon's dog-men (Judges 6:11–7:23).**
God chooses Gideon to lead an army against the Midianites. Gideon gathers an army of 32,000 men, but this is too many. God tells Gideon to make all the men drink from a stream, and then selects only the 300 men who lap water like dogs.

❷ **David ambushes Saul in a cave while he's "busy" (1 Samuel 24:2–7).**
While pursuing David cross-country to engage him in battle, Saul goes into a cave to "relieve himself" (move his bowels). Unbeknownst to Saul, David and his men are already hiding in the very same cave. While Saul's doing his business, David sneaks up and cuts off a corner of Saul's cloak with a knife. Outside afterward, David shows King Saul the piece of cloth to prove he could have killed him "on the throne."

❸ **King David does the goofy (2 Samuel 6:14).**
David is so excited about bringing the Ark of the Covenant to Jerusalem that he dances before God and all the people dressed only in a linen ephod, an apron-like garment that covered only the front of his body.

❹ Lot's wife (Genesis 19:24–26).
While fleeing God's wrath upon the cities of Sodom and Gomorrah, Lot's wife forgets (or ignores) God's warning not to look back upon the destruction and turns into a woman-sized pillar of salt.

❺ Gerasene demoniac (Mark 5:1–20).
A man is possessed by so many demons that chains cannot hold him. Jesus exorcises the demons and sends them into a herd of 2,000 pigs, which then run over the edge of a cliff and drown in the sea. The herders, now 2,000 pigs poorer, get miffed and ask Jesus to leave.

❻ Disciples and loaves of bread (Mark 8:14–21).
The disciples were there when Jesus fed 5,000 people with just five loaves of bread and two fish. They also saw him feed 4,000 people with seven loaves. Later, in a boat, the disciples fret to an exasperated Jesus because they have only one loaf for 13 people.

❼ Peter can't swim (Matthew 14:22–33).
Blundering Peter sees Jesus walking on the water and wants to join him. But when the wind picks up, Peter panics and starts to sink. In Greek, the name Peter means "rock."

Peter, "the rock," sank when he looked to himself instead of to Jesus. Jesus later described Peter as a Rock of the church (Matthew 16:18).

Bible Stuff

THE FIVE GROSSEST BIBLE STORIES

❶ Eglon and Ehud (Judges 3:12–30).
Before kings reigned over Israel, judges ruled the people. At that time, a very overweight king named Eglon conquered Israel and demanded money. A man named Ehud brought the payment to Eglon while he was perched on his "throne" (meaning "toilet"). Along with the money, Ehud handed over a little something extra—his sword, which he buried so far in Eglon's belly that the sword disappeared into the king's fat and, as the Bible says, "the dirt came out" (v. 22).

❷ Job's sores (Job 2:1–10).
Job lived a righteous life yet he suffered anyway. He had oozing sores from the bald spot on top of his head clear down to the soft spot on the bottom of his foot. Job used a broken piece of pottery to scrape away the pus that leaked from his sores.

❸ The naked prophet (Isaiah 20).
God's prophets went to great lengths to get God's message across to the people. Isaiah was no exception. God's people planned a war, but God gave it the thumbs down. Isaiah marched around Jerusalem naked *for three years* as a sign of what would happen if the people went to war.

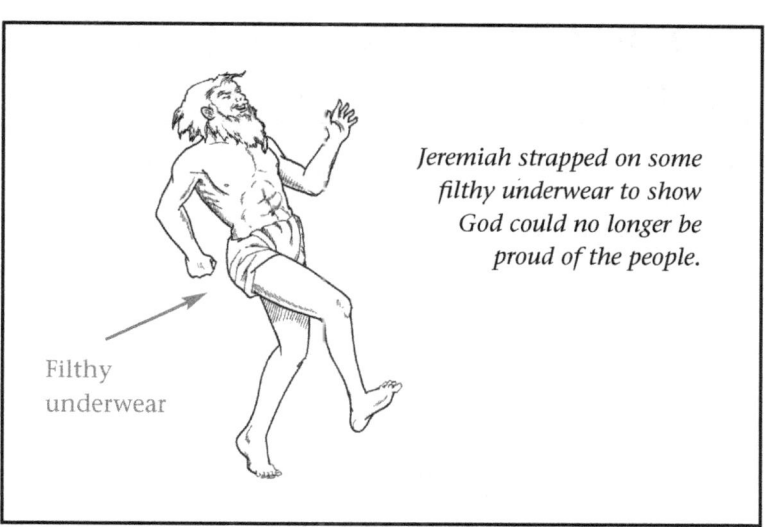

Jeremiah strapped on some filthy underwear to show God could no longer be proud of the people.

Filthy underwear

❹ The almost-naked prophet (Jeremiah 13:1–11).
God sent Jeremiah to announce that God could no longer be proud of the people. To make the point, Jeremiah bought a new pair of underclothes, wore them every day without washing them, then buried them in the wet river sand. Later, he dug them up, strapped them on, and shouted that this is what has happened to the people who were God's pride!

❺ Spilling your guts (Matthew 27:1–8; Acts 1:16–19).
Judas betrayed Jesus and sold him out for 30 pieces of silver. He bought a field with the ill-gotten loot. Guilt-stricken, Judas walked out to the field, his belly swelled up until it burst, and his intestines spilled out on to the ground.

FIVE FACTS ABOUT LIFE IN OLD TESTAMENT TIMES

❶ Almost everyone wore sandals.
They were called *sandals* because people walked on sand much of the time.

❷ There were no newspapers.
People got news by hearing it from other people. Spreading important news was like a giant game of "telephone."

❸ It was dark.
Homes, often tents, were typically lit at night by an oil lamp, if at all.

❹ You had to fetch your water, which was scarce.
Rich folks had servants to carry it for them, but most people had to carry household water in jugs or leather bags, usually some distance, from a river or well.

❺ Life expectancy was short.
Despite some long-lived exceptions described in the book of Genesis, such as Abraham (175 years) and Methuselah (969 years), few people lived past 50.

Sandals were made for walking on sand.

TEN IMPORTANT THINGS THAT HAPPENED BETWEEN THE OLD AND NEW TESTAMENTS

The period of time described in the Old Testament ended about 400 years before Jesus' birth. The people of God kept living, believing, struggling, and writing during that period. Here are some of the important events that took place between the Testaments.

❶ The Hebrew nation dissolved.

In the Old Testament, at the end of the book of 2 Kings, the Babylonians destroyed Jerusalem and Solomon's temple, and took the leaders into exile. This happened in 587 B.C. Over the next centuries, many different kingdoms and empires controlled Jerusalem.

❷ The people scattered.

After the exile to Babylon ended, the people of Judah moved to many different places. Some of them later came back, but many never did. Some of them lived in Babylon, some lived in Egypt, and some just scattered elsewhere.

❸ A religion replaced a nation.

As a result of items 1 and 2, the people's religion changed. They no longer had a state or national religion (Judean religion). Instead, they had a freestanding faith called Judaism.

Bible Stuff

❹ **The Aramaic language became popular.**
Because Aramaic was the international language of the Persian Empire, many Jews quit speaking Hebrew and spoke Aramaic instead. This is why Jesus spoke Aramaic.

❺ **Alexander the Great conquered the world.**
Around 330 B.C., Alexander the Great conquered the Mediterranean and Mesopotamian world. As a result, Greek became the everyday language of business and trade in the region. This is why the New Testament was written in Greek.

❻ **The hammer dropped.**
Around 170 B.C., the Greek emperor outlawed circumcision and the Sabbath, and defiled the temple. A family of Jews called the Maccabees (which means "hammer") led a revolt.

❼ **The Hebrew Scriptures were finished.**
During this time, the individual books that make up what we call the Old Testament were finished. Several other religious books written at this time (mostly in Greek) aren't in the Protestant Bible but are part of the Apocrypha.

❽ **The Sadducees, Pharisees, Essenes, Samaritans, Zealots, and other groups of people sprouted up.**
Different schools of thought developed within Judaism. Most of their disagreements were over the idea that God's people would be resurrected to eternal life.

⑨ David's descendants weren't kings.
God promised King David that one of his descendants would always be king in Jerusalem. But after the Babylonian exile, David's heirs faded from view. Some people wondered what had happened to God's promise.

⑩ The Roman Empire expanded.
In 63 B.C., the Roman Empire conquered Palestine, having already conquered pretty much everyone else in the region. This is why the Roman Empire ruled the area during the time of Jesus and the New Testament.

FIVE FACTS ABOUT LIFE IN NEW TESTAMENT TIMES

❶ There were no church buildings.
For worship, Jesus' people gathered in all kinds of places, often outdoors. *Church* was any gathering of people for worship.

❷ Houses were boxy.
Most houses had a flat roof with an outside staircase leading to it. Inhabitants would sleep on the roof during hot weather.

Houses in New Testament times were boxy.

❸ Every town had a marketplace.
Usually there was just one marketplace per town, but one could buy almost everything needed to live.

❹ People ate a lot of fish.
The most common fish in the Sea of Galilee were catfish and carp. Roasting over a charcoal fire was the most common method of cooking.

❺ Dogs were shunned.
The Jewish people in Jesus' day did not keep dogs as pets. Dogs were considered unclean because they ate garbage and animal carcasses.

THE FIVE BIGGEST MISCONCEPTIONS ABOUT THE BIBLE

❶ The Bible was written in a short period of time.
Christians believe that God inspired the Bible writers, the first of whom may have been Moses. God inspired people to write down important histories, traditions, songs, wise sayings, poetry, and prophetic words. All told—from the first recordings of the stories in Genesis to the last decisions about Revelation—the entire Bible formed over a period spanning anywhere from 800 to 1,400 years!

❷ One person wrote the Bible.
Unlike Islam's Koran, which was written by the prophet Muhammad, the books of the Bible claim the handiwork of many people. Much of Scripture does not identify the human hand that wrote it, so some parts of the Bible may have been written by women as well as men.

❸ The entire Bible should be taken literally.
While many parts of the Bible are meant as descriptions of actual historical events, other parts are intended as *illustrations of God's truth*, such as Song of Solomon, the book of Revelation, and Jesus' parable of the good Samaritan. So when Jesus says, "If your right eye causes you to sin, tear it out and throw it away" (Matthew 5:29), please do not take the saying literally!

④ **People in Bible times were unenlightened.**
During the 1,400 years it took to write the Bible, some of history's greatest thinkers lived and worked. Many of these philosophers, architects, mathematicians, orators, theologians, historians, doctors, military tacticians, inventors, engineers, poets, and playwrights are still quoted today and their works are still in use.

⑤ **The Bible is a single book.**
The Bible is actually a collection of books, letters, and other writings—more like a library than a book. There are 39 books in the Hebrew Scriptures, what Christians call the "Old" Testament, and 27 books (mostly letters) in the New Testament. There are seven books in the Apocrypha (books written between the Old and New Testaments), or "deuterocanonical" books.

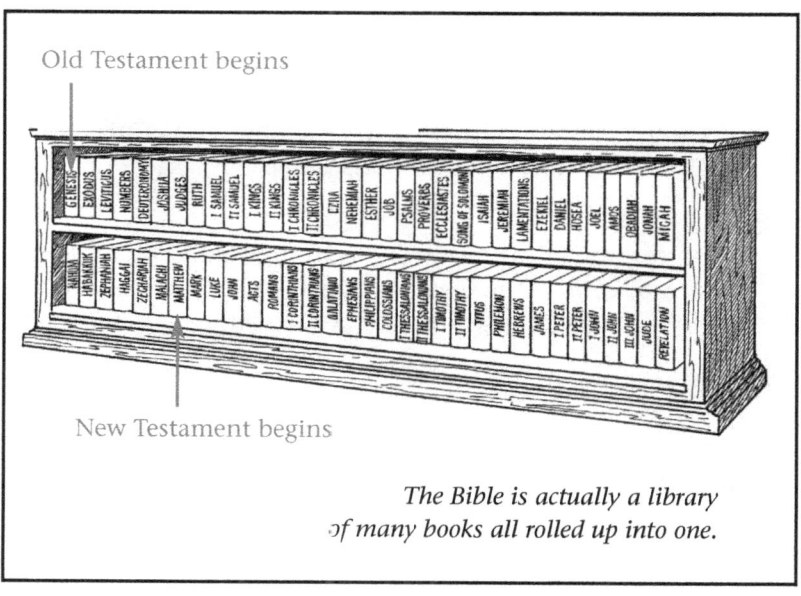

The Bible is actually a library of many books all rolled up into one.

Bible Stuff

JESUS' TWELVE APOSTLES (PLUS JUDAS AND PAUL)

While Jesus had many disciples (students and followers), the Bible focuses particularly on twelve who were closest to him. Tradition says that these twelve spread Jesus' message throughout the known world (Matthew 28:18–20). For this reason, they were known as *apostles*, a word that means "sent ones."

❶ Andrew
A fisherman and the first disciple to follow Jesus, Andrew brought his brother, Simon Peter, to Jesus.

❷ Bartholomew
Also called Nathanael, tradition has it that he was martyred by being skinned alive.

❸ James the Elder
James, with John and Peter, was one of Jesus' closest disciples. Herod Agrippa killed James because of his faith, which made him a martyr (Acts 12:2).

❹ John
John (or one of his followers) is traditionally thought to be the author of the Gospel of John and the three letters of John. He probably died of natural causes in old age.

❺ Matthew
Matthew was a tax collector and, therefore, probably an outcast even among his own people. He is traditionally attributed with the authorship of the Gospel of Matthew.

⑥ Peter
Peter was a fisherman who was brought to faith by his brother Andrew. He was probably martyred in Rome by being crucified upside down.

⑦ Philip
Philip, possibly a Greek, is responsible for bringing Bartholomew (Nathanael) to faith. He is thought to have died in a city called Phrygia.

⑧ James the Less
James was called "the Less" so he wouldn't be confused with James, the brother of John, or James, Jesus' brother.

⑨ Simon
Simon is often called "the Zealot." Zealots were a political group in Jesus' day that favored the overthrow of the Roman government by force.

⑩ Jude
Jude may have worked with Simon the Zealot in Persia (Iran) where they were martyred on the same day.

⑪ Thomas
It is thought that "doubting" Thomas preached the message of Jesus in India.

⑫ Matthias
Matthias was chosen by lot to replace Judas. It is thought that he worked mostly in Ethiopia.

⑬ Judas Iscariot

Judas was the treasurer for Jesus' disciples and the one who betrayed Jesus for 30 pieces of silver. According to the Bible, Judas killed himself for his betrayal.

⑭ Paul

Paul is considered primarily responsible for bringing non-Jewish people to faith in Jesus. He traveled extensively and wrote many letters to believers. Many of Paul's letters are included in the New Testament.

THE FIVE WEIRDEST LAWS IN THE OLD TESTAMENT

The Old Testament has many helpful, common sense laws, such as "You shall not kill," and, "You shall not steal." But there are a few others that need some explaining.

❶ The "ox" law.

"When an ox gores a man or a woman to death, the ox shall be stoned, and its flesh shall not be eaten; but the owner of the ox shall not be liable" (Exodus 21:28). Replace "ox" with "car" and the law makes more sense—it is about protecting others from reckless actions.

People living in biblical times were sometimes gored by oxen.

Bible Stuff

People who were gored by oxen—or victims of other crimes—had legal recourse.

② **The "no kid boiling" law.**
"You shall not boil a kid in its mother's milk" (Exodus 23:19b). A "kid," of course, is a juvenile goat, not a human being.

③ **The "which bugs are legal to eat" law.**
"All winged insects that walk upon all fours are detestable to you. But among the winged insects that walk on all fours you may eat those that have jointed legs above their feet" (Leviticus 11:20–21). The law is unclear whether it is legal to eat the bug if you first pull off the legs.

④ **The "don't eat blood" law.**
"No person among you shall eat blood" (Leviticus 17:12). Some laws beg the question whether people in that time had any sense of taste.

⑤ **The "pure cloth" law.**
"You shall not wear clothes made of wool and linen woven together" (Deuteronomy 22:11). Polyester came along after Bible times.

THE TOP TEN BIBLE MIRACLES AND WHAT THEY MEAN

❶ Creation.
God created the universe and everything that is in it, and God continues to create and re-create without ceasing. God's first and ongoing miracle was to reveal that the creation has a purpose.

❷ The Passover.
The Israelites were enslaved by Pharaoh, a ruler who believed the people belonged to him, not to God. In the last of ten plagues, God visited the houses of all the Egyptians to kill the firstborn male in each one. God alone is Lord of the people, and no human can claim ultimate power over us.

❸ The Exodus.
God's people were fleeing Egypt when Pharaoh dispatched his army to force them back into slavery. The army trapped the people with their backs to a sea, but God parted the water and the people walked across to freedom while Pharaoh's minions were destroyed. God chose to free us from all forms of tyranny so we may use that freedom to serve God and each other.

❹ Manna.
After the people crossed the sea to freedom, they complained that they were going to starve to death. They even asked to go back to Egypt. God sent manna, a form of bread, so the people lived. God cares for us even when we give up, pine for our slavery, and lose faith. God never abandons us.

❺ The Incarnation.
The immortal and infinite God became a human being, choosing to be born of a woman. God loved us enough to become one of us in Jesus of Nazareth, forever bridging the divide that had separated us from God.

❻ Jesus healed the paralyzed man.
Some men brought a paralyzed friend to Jesus. Jesus said, "Son, your sins are forgiven" (Mark 2:5). This means that Jesus has the power to forgive our sins—and he does so as a free gift.

❼ Jesus calmed the storm.
Jesus was asleep in a boat with his disciples when a great storm came up and threatened to sink it. He said, "Peace! Be still!" (Mark 4:39). Then the storm immediately calmed. Jesus is Lord over even the powers of nature.

❽ The Resurrection.
Human beings executed Jesus, but God raised him from the dead on the third day. Through baptism, we share in Jesus' death, so we will also share in eternal life with God the Father, Son, and Holy Spirit. Christ conquered death.

❾ Pentecost.
Jesus ascended from the earth, but he did not leave the church powerless or alone. On the 50th day after the Jewish Passover (*Pentecost* means 50th), Jesus sent the Holy Spirit to create the church and take up residence among us. The Holy Spirit is present with us always.

❿ The Second Coming.
One day, Christ will come again and end all suffering. This means that the final result of the epic battle between good and evil is already assured. It is simply that evil has not yet admitted defeat.

THE EXODUS

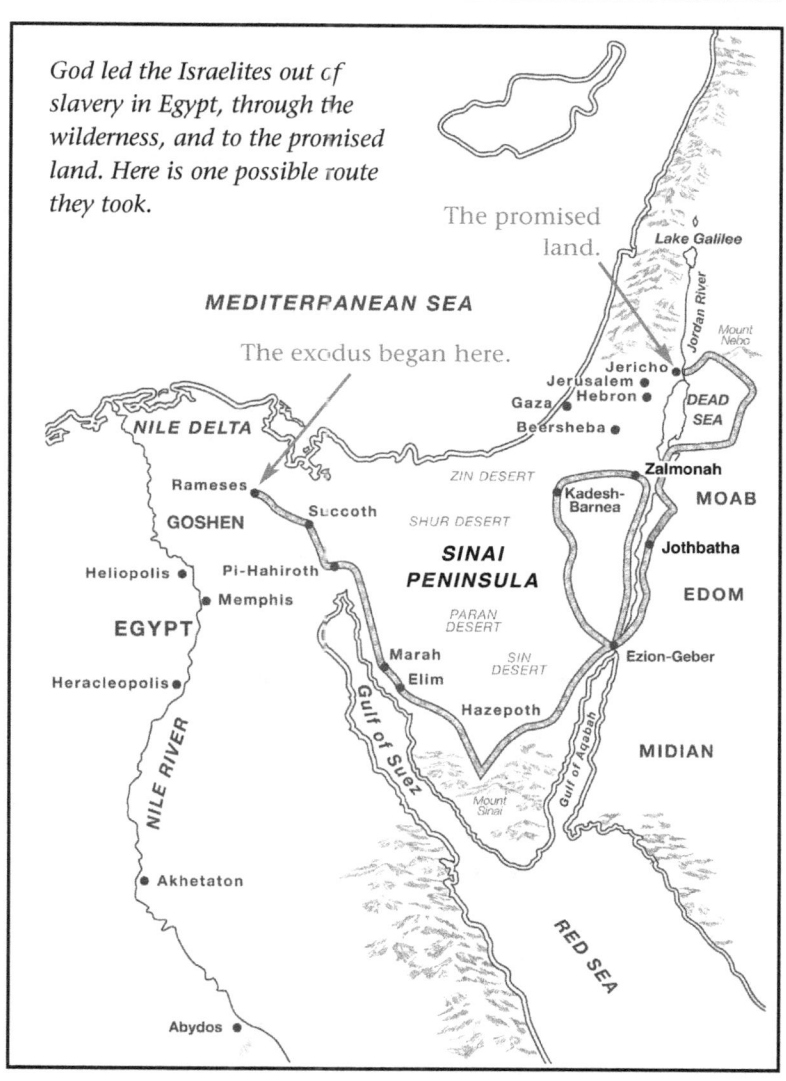

THE HOLY LAND—
OLD TESTAMENT TIMES

THE HOLY LAND—
NEW TESTAMENT TIMES

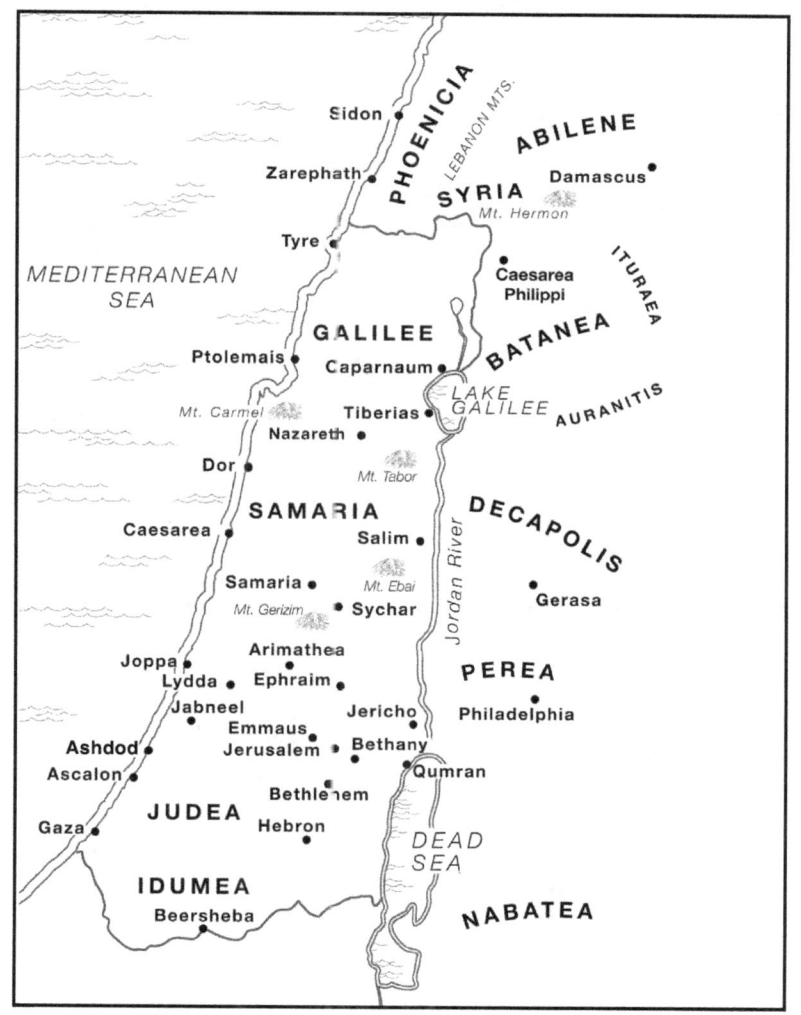

PAUL'S JOURNEYS

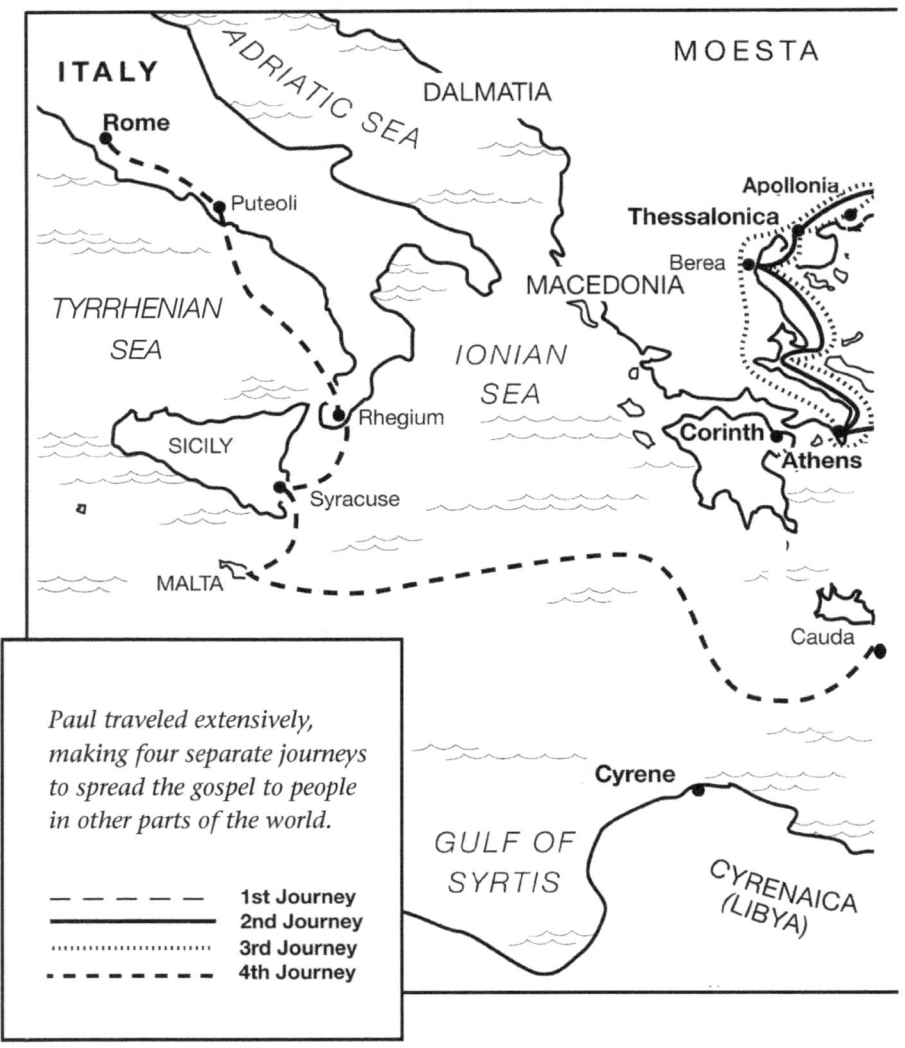

Paul traveled extensively, making four separate journeys to spread the gospel to people in other parts of the world.

― ― ― ― ― 1st Journey
─────── 2nd Journey
.... 3rd Journey
‐ ‐ ‐ ‐ ‐ ‐ 4th Journey

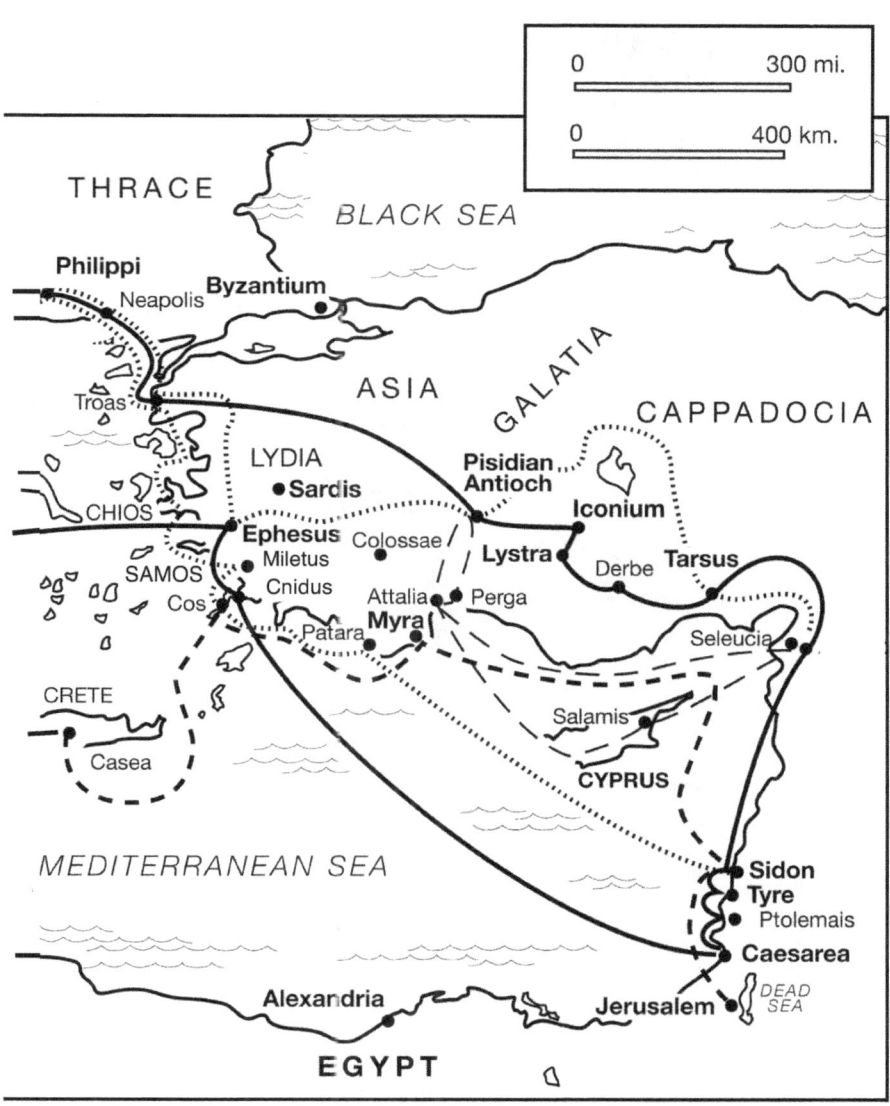

JERUSALEM IN JESUS' TIME

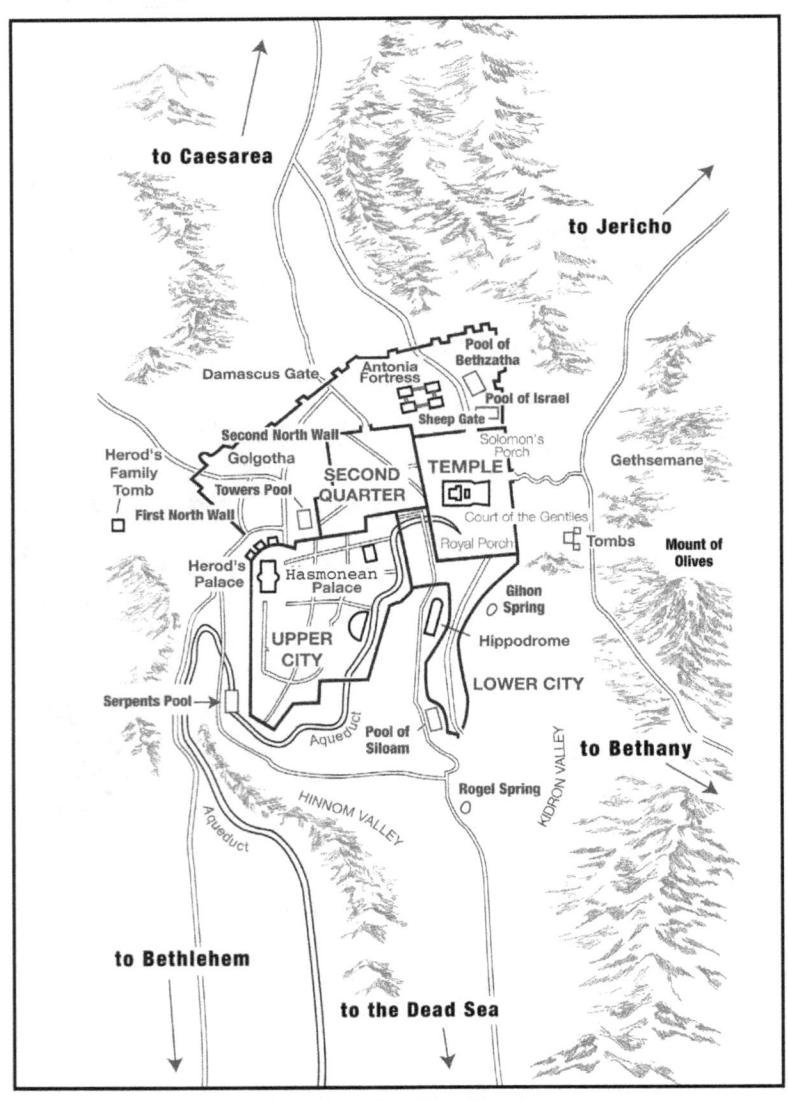

NOAH'S ARK

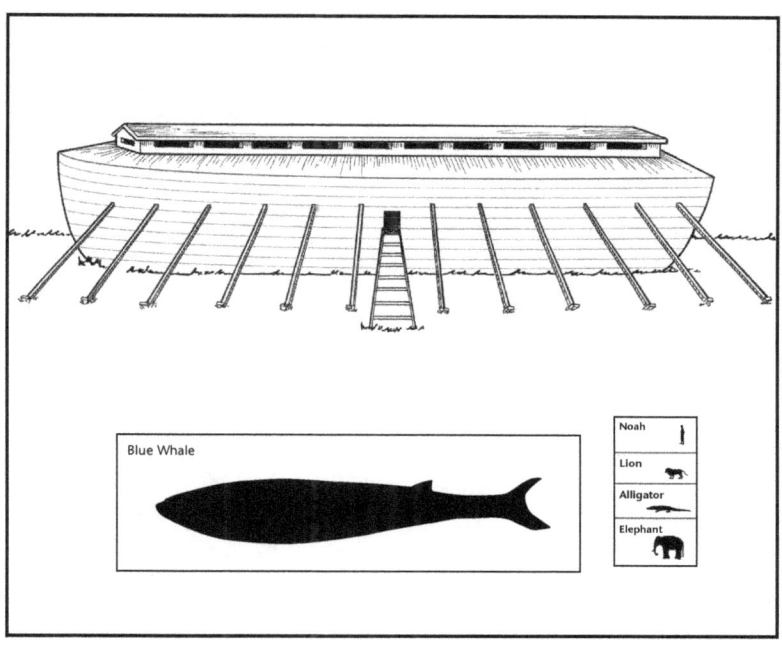

A cubit is equal to the length of a man's forearm from the elbow to the tip of the middle finger—approximately 18 inches or 45.7 centimeters. Noah's ark was 300 cubits long, 50 cubits wide, and 30 cubits tall (Genesis 6:15).

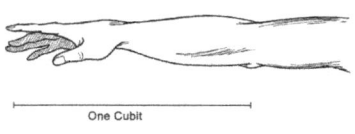

Bible Stuff

THE ARK OF THE COVENANT

God told the Israelites to place the stone tablets—the "covenant"—of the law into the Ark of the Covenant. The Israelites believed that God was invisibly enthroned above the vessel and went before them wherever they traveled.

The Ark of the Covenant was 2.5 cubits long and 1.5 cubits wide (Exodus 25:10).

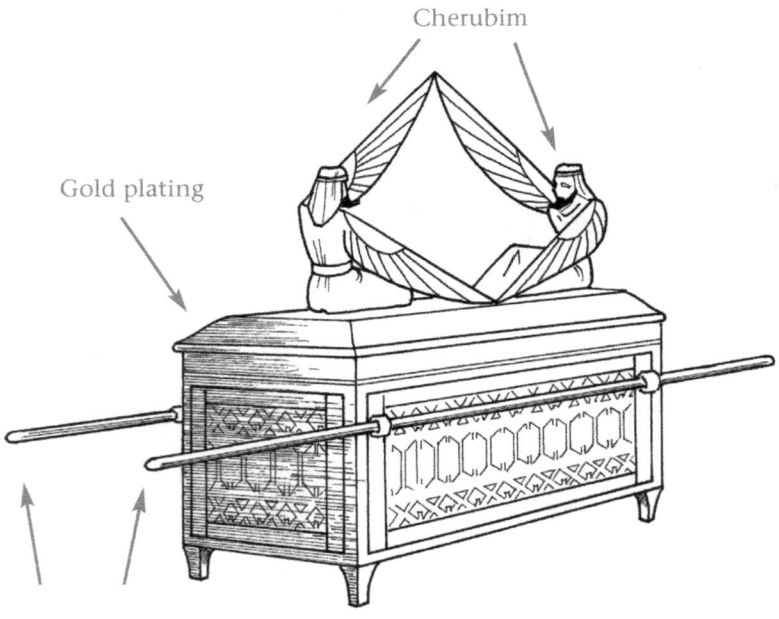

Cherubim

Gold plating

Carrying poles

Exodus 25:10–22

SOLOMON'S TEMPLE

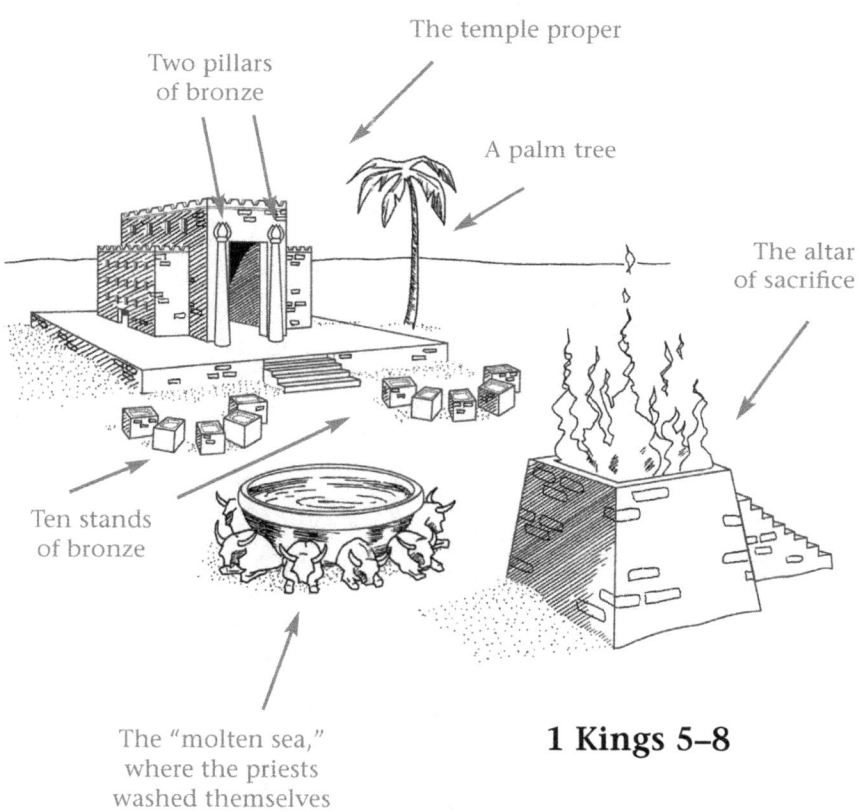

Two pillars of bronze

The temple proper

A palm tree

The altar of sacrifice

Ten stands of bronze

The "molten sea," where the priests washed themselves

1 Kings 5–8

Bible Stuff

THE ARMOR OF GOD

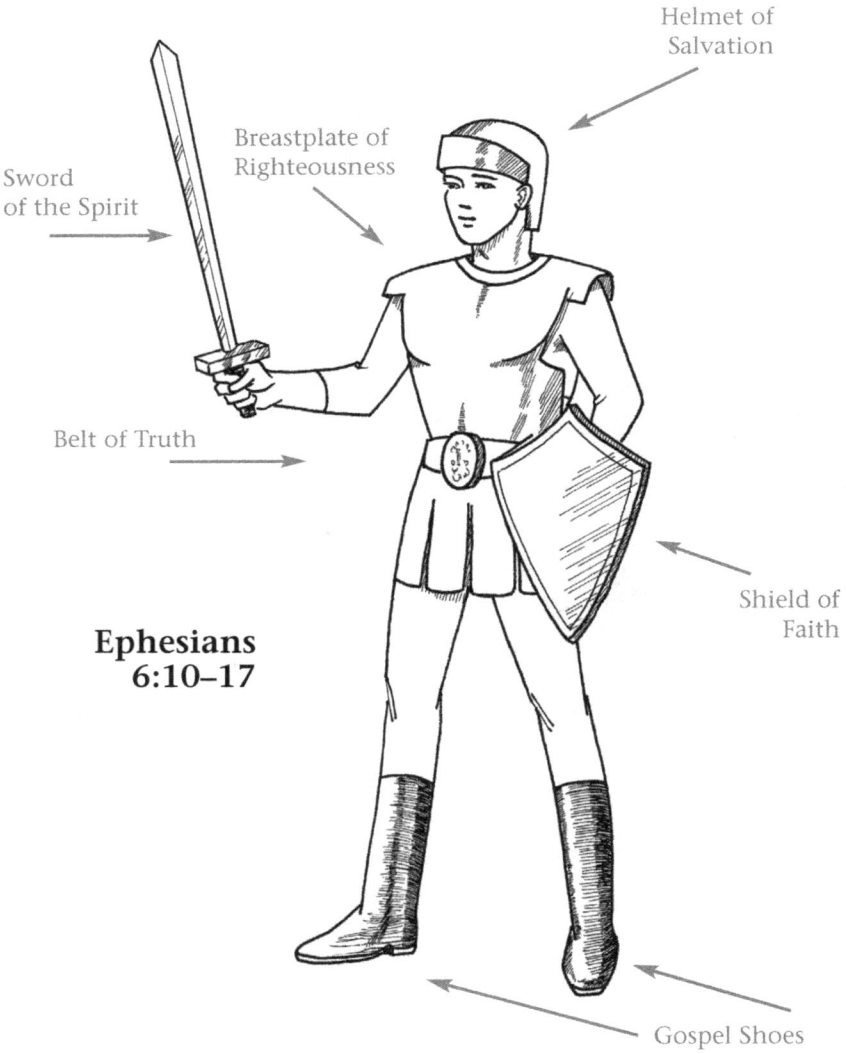

THE CRUCIFIXION

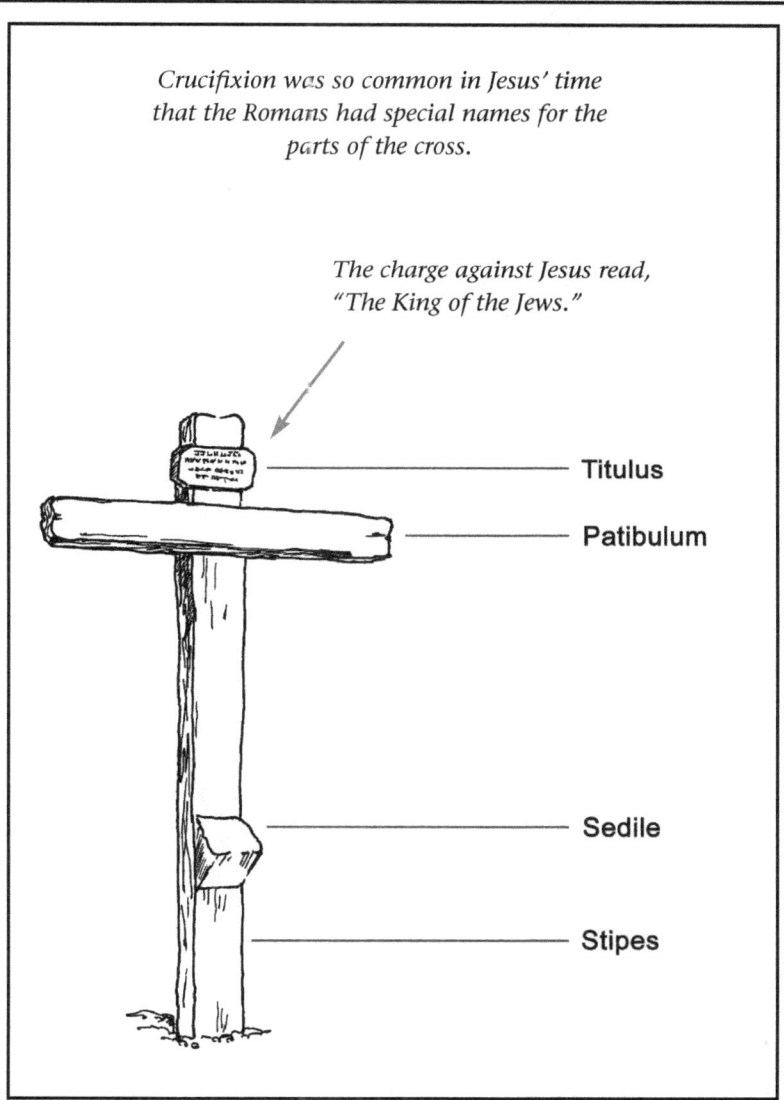

Crucifixion was so common in Jesus' time that the Romans had special names for the parts of the cross.

The charge against Jesus read, "The King of the Jews."

— Titulus
— Patibulum
— Sedile
— Stipes

Bible Stuff

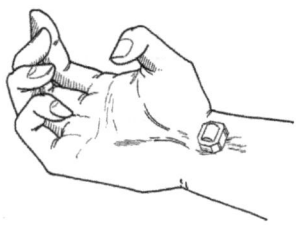
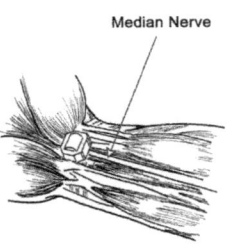

Typical crucifixion involved being nailed to the cross through the wrists—an excruciatingly painful and humiliating punishment.

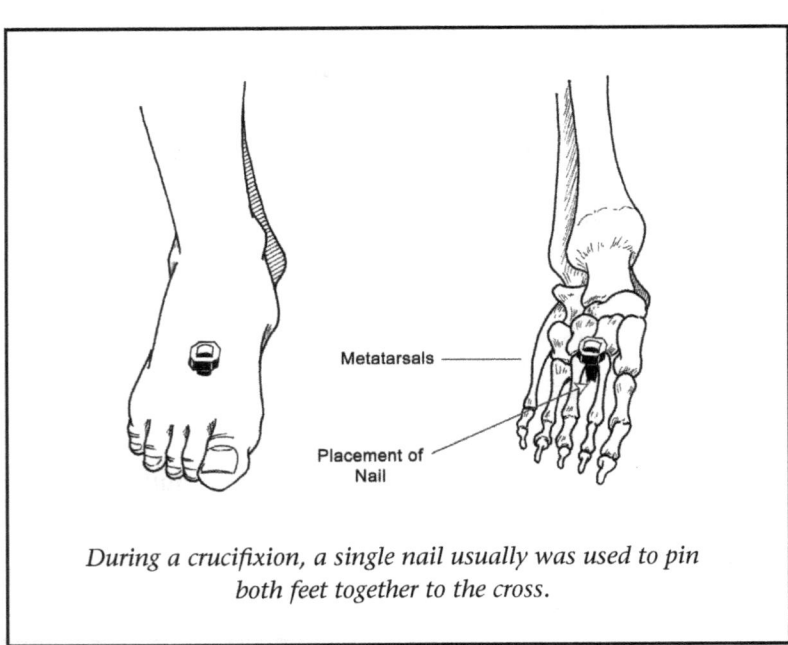

During a crucifixion, a single nail usually was used to pin both feet together to the cross.

Eventually, the victim would be unable to lift himself to take a breath, and he would suffocate.

While the Romans broke the legs of the men who were crucified next to Jesus, they found that Jesus had already died. To make sure, one pierced his side with a spear, probably to puncture his heart (John 19:34).

Bible Stuff

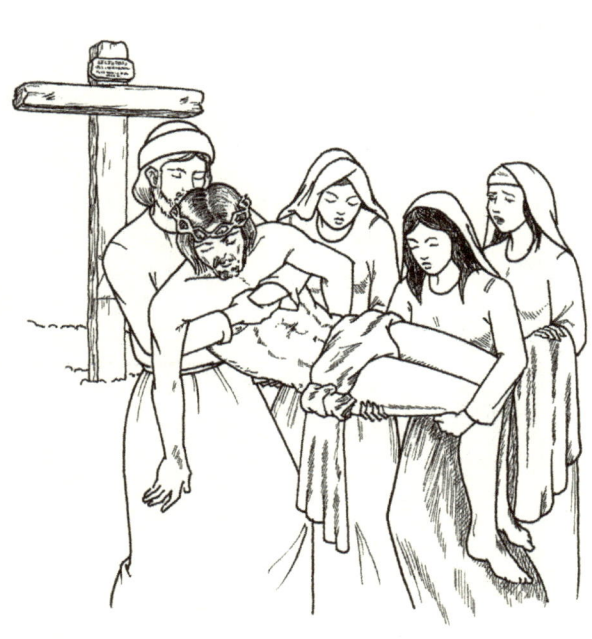

Joseph of Arimathea and several women took Jesus down and carried him to the tomb (Matthew 27:57–61).

The miracle of resurrection took place three days later, when Jesus rose from the dead.

CUMBERLAND PRESBYTERIAN STUFF

Being Cumberland Presbyterian is a way of being Christian. *Cumberland Presbyterian* is more like an adjective than a noun. We are *Cumberland Presbyterian Christians*.

But Cumberland Presbyterians have their own history, theological emphases, and ways of being Christian in the world. To be a Cumberland Presbyterian means you are inserted into a family of faith that has expressed its faith and practiced being Christians in certain, recognizable ways and patterns throughout the centuries.

We celebrate our identity as Cumberland Presbyterian Christians. We are grateful that God has called us into this family of faith and that we have expressed our faith in important ways. Our Cumberland Presbyterian heritage can help us live as faithful Christians in the years ahead.

THE CHURCH ON A MISSION FROM GOD

The Church has Purpose

Cumberland Presbyterians recognize that the church is the people of God who serve God in this world through Jesus Christ by the power of the Holy Spirit.

We believe that God created the church for special purposes:

- to be a community of love.

- to proclaim the gospel through worship and the sacraments.

- to reach out to those who have not experienced God's grace in Christ.

- to enable deeds of service and mercy in the world.

- to minister to the needs of persons and promote social righteousness.

THE CHURCH REFORMED AND ALWAYS BEING REFORMED

A motto that came to be associated with Reformed churches during and after the Reformation is the Latin phrase *Ecclesia reformata, semper reformanda*. It means "The church reformed, always being reformed." This motto does not sanction change in the church, just for the sake of change; nor does it seek preservation of the past only for the sake of preservation.

In Reformation times, Christians who used this phrase stressed that the church was to return to the model of the church found in Scripture without the "innovations" that had emerged through the centuries in the Roman Catholic Church. The church "reformed."

The church, however, is also to be open to the new changes that God wants to bring about for the church in the future. The church must always be ready to "be reformed."

Often, there was another phrase added to this motto: "according to Scripture." The church is to be "reformed" on the basis of Scripture; the church is to be open to the reform God wants, on the basis of Scripture.

So, this motto challenges both liberals and conservatives in the church. We maintain continuity with our past, but are open to the future to which God calls us, as the church listens to Scripture and is led by the Holy Spirit.

KEY CUMBERLAND PRESBYTERIAN CONCEPTS

There are some themes that have been particular emphases of Cumberland Presbyterians and the Reformed tradition. These are not the sole property of the Reformed! But they mark themes that have been especially important for Reformed churches.

These can be summarized and expanded as:

- **Sovereignty.** God is the majestic, holy God who creates, sustains, rules, and redeems the world. God's providence is God's guidance and work in history and in the lives of individuals.
- **Grace.** God's primary attitude toward all of creation. *Grace* is the love and mercy God show us when we don't deserve it. Even God's discipline is rooted in God's desire to maintain the relationship.
- **Covenant.** God enters into a relationship with people: Israel in the Old Testament; the church in the New Testament. They are the people of God who proclaim and seek to order their lives by God's Word.
- **Stewardship.** The people of God manage God's gifts responsibly and seek to make proper use of the good gifts of God's creation.
- **Sin.** Humans often fail to see themselves as God sees them: as beloved creatures made in God's image, created for relationship with God and one another. This broken relationship is sin.

- **Repentance.** God offers all human beings an opportunity to recognize sin, turn away from it and live gratefully in obedience to God. The capacity for repentance is itself a gift of God's grace, the Holy Spirit working wihin us.
- **Obedience.** The people of God work for justice and social transformation as expressions of their obedience to God's Word and will in Jesus Christ.

CHURCH GOVERNMENT

The term *polity* means "government" and Presbyterian polity is the form of government by which the Cumberland Presbyterian Church operates.

❶ The Confession of Faith and Government

The Cumberland Presbyterian Church is governed by a *Confession of Faith and Government*. It has five parts.

The Confession of Faith. The doctrinal statements that convey what the church believes.

The Constitution. The policies and procedures of the church that enable it to carry out its ministries.

The Rules of Discipline. The policies and procedures to help the church respond when problems arise.

The Directory for Worship. Guidelines for ordering the corporate worship of God.

The Rules of Order. The procedures that guide meetings of church governing bodies—sort of a *Robert's Rules of Order Lite*.

❷ The Governing Structures

The church is governed by representatives and has a graduated system of governing bodies. These are sometimes seen to correspond to the structures of the United States government.

Church	U.S.A.
Session	City
Presbytery	County
Synod	State
General Assembly	National

CHURCH LINGO

Cumberland Presbyterians use words to describe their church lives and practices. Some are specialized terms. Here is a sampling.

- **General Assembly.** The church's highest governing body, meeting annually, and including elder and clergy commissioners from all the denomination's presbyteries.
- **Synod.** The church's governing body beyond the presbytery level, embracing presbyteries from a specific geographical region.
- **Presbytery.** The church's key governing body composed of clergy and elected lay leaders (elders) in a specific geographical area.
- **Local church.** The individual congregation to which people belong. The Constitution calls this a "particular church," but most people refer to a congregation as a "local church."
- **Elder.** An elected representative in a local church who is ordained to carry out duties of governing and spiritual care.
- **Session.** The group of elders who have spiritual and governmental oversight in a local church.
- **Stated Clerk.** The person who functions as the official record keeper and in some cases the spokesperson for a governing body such as a presbytery, a synod, or the General Assembly.
- **Clerk of Session.** The official record keeper for the session in a local church.
- **Deacon.** An ordained office in a local church charged with ministries of care, witness, and service.

ORDINATION AND INSTALLATION

Ordination is a biblical practice of setting a person apart for a form of ministry or service to God. The church ordains leaders who will serve the church in various ways.

The Cumberland Presbyterian Church ordains people to these "offices" in the church. Ordinations take place in the midst of worship services and are accompanied by prayer and the laying on of hands

- Deacons
- Elders
- Ministers of the Word and Sacrament

Installation is a service in the midst of worship for those previously ordained who have been called anew to serve as deacons, elders, or ministers of Word and Sacrament.

CONFESSING THE FAITH

The psalmist in the Old Testament said, "Let the redeemed of the Lord say so" (Psalm 107:2)!

People of faith throughout the Bible—and beyond—have always felt the need to express their experience of God in words. Early followers of Jesus told the stories of Jesus far and wide. The early church spread throughout the ancient world as Christians proclaimed their belief in Jesus of Nazareth as God's son, our Savior, the Messiah. This was a wonderful message—the gospel message—that was preached and taught by ordinary Christian believers who found their lives were changed forever because of their faith in Jesus Christ.

Cumberland Presbyterians have been eager to express their Christian faith. We have done so in many ways, one of the most important being by the use of creeds and confessions. All human language is pressed into the service of proclaiming the "good news of great joy for all the people" (Luke 2:10)—the message of Jesus Christ!

CREEDS AND CONFESSIONS

A characteristic of Presbyterian and Reformed Christians is their conviction that Christian faith should be confessed. We are a confessional people. Wherever new Reformed and Presbyterian churches have emerged, new confessions of faith (or creeds) have followed. Confessions of faith are ways of expressing what Christians believe the Bible teaches. Cumberland Presbyterians believe God wants us to witness to the faith in which we believe and to commend this faith to others by preaching and teaching and proclaiming. Confessions of faith provide a means to help churches define and implement their ministries.

Creeds or confessions of faith vary in terms of their purposes, forms, and functions.

- **Short summaries.** The Apostles' Creed and Nicene Creed are short summaries of Christian belief.
- **Comprehensive statements.** Many confessions of faith are detailed expositions of Christian theology. They cover many doctrines. Examples are the Second Helvetic Confession (1566) and the Westminster Confession of Faith (1647).
- **Specific issues.** Sometimes the church is impelled to confess its faith in the midst of specific crises or problems by witnessing to the gospel. The threat of Nazism led to the Theological Declaration of Barmen (1934).

> **Creed**—(Latin *credo*: "I believe.")
> A creed is a formal, authorized confession of important points of Christian doctrine or teaching.

THE *CONFESSION OF FAITH*

Cumberland Presbyterians think having a *Confession of Faith* is important for a couple of reasons: it gives people who already trust God for their salvation a way to understand and talk about their faith; it serves as a witness to the gospel of salvation through Jesus Christ for people who have not yet believed.

Because we think it is important to be "Reformed and always being reformed," Cumberland Presbyterians have adopted new confessional statements at different points in our history. We have wanted to express our ancient, biblical faith in fresh contemporary language.

The current *Confession of Faith* was adopted in 1984 by the General Assemblies of both the Cumberland Presbyterian Church and the Cumberland Presbyterian Church in America. Members of both denominations were instrumental in shaping it.

The Cumberland Presbyterian Church has used four different confessions throughout our history:

- The Westminster Confession of Faith (1647; England)
- The Confession of Faith (1814; United States)
- The Confession of Faith (1883; United States)
- The Confession of Faith (1984; United States)

KEY COMMENTS FROM THE CONFESSION

The *Confession of Faith (COF)* contains many penetrating and comforting theological insights. Here are some of the important statements from the 1984 Cumberland Presbyterian confession.

- **About God**

    By word and action God invites persons into a covenant relationship. God promises to be faithful to the covenant and to make all who believe his people. All who respond with trust and commitment to God's invitation find the promise sure and rejoice in being members of God's people, the covenant community.—1.03 *(COF)*

- **About Scripture**

    In order to understand God's word spoken in and through the scriptures, persons must have the illumination of God's own spirit. Moreover, they should study the writings of the Bible in their historical settings, compare scripture with scripture, listen to the witness of the church throughout the centuries, and share insights with others in the covenant community.—1.07 *(COF)*

- **About God's Will**

    God's will is sufficiently disclosed for persons to respond to it in worship, love, and service, yet they should hold in reverence and wonder the mystery of divine ways.—1.09 *(COF)*

- **About Providence**

    God's providence is sufficiently displayed to be known and experienced, but, at the same time, it partakes of divine mystery, and is the occasion for wonder, praise, and thanksgiving. Thus even in illness, pain, sorrow, tragedy, social upheaval, or natural disaster, persons may be sure of God's presence and discover his grace to be sufficient.—1.18 *(COF)*

- **About Human Freedom**

    God, in creating persons, gives them the capacity and freedom to respond to divine grace in loving obedience. Therefore, whoever will may be saved.—2.01 *(COF)*

- **About God's Covenant**

    God's covenant is a relationship of grace. It appears in various forms and manifestations in the scripures but always as one of grace The new covenant in Jesus Christ is its ultimate and supreme expression.—3.03 *(COF)*

- **About the Holy Spirit**

    God acted redemptively in Jesus Christ because of the sins of the world and continues with the same intent in the Holy Spirit to call every person to repentance and faith.—4.01 *(COF)*

- **About Regeneration and Adoption**

    All persons dying in infancy and all who have never had the ability to respond to Christ are regenerated and saved by God's grace.—4.19 *(COF)*

- **About Worship**

    Christian worship is the affirmation of God's living presence and the celebration of God's mighty acts. It is central to the life of the church and is the appropriate response of all believers to the lordship and sovereignty of God.—5.12 *(COF)*

- **About the Church in Mission**

    The covenant community is responsible to give witness

to the mighty acts of God in the life, death, and resurrection of Jesus Christ. Where and when this witness is lacking, God is not without a witness. Therefore, it does not belong to the covenant community to judge where and in what manner God acts savingly through Jesus Christ.—5.31 *(COF)*

- **About Stewardship**

    Christian stewardship acknowledges that all of life and creation is a trust from God, to be used for God's glory and service. It includes the conservation and responsible use of natural resources as well as the creative use of human skills and energies. These gifts of God are to be shared with all, especially with the poor.—6.10 *(COF)*

- **About Judgment and Consummation**

    In the consummation of history, at the coming of Jesus Christ, the kingdoms of the world shall become the kingdom of the Lord and of the Christ, and he shall reign forever and ever.—7.08 *(COF)*

TIPS ON INTERPRETING THE *CONFESSION OF FAITH*

Compared to the doctrinal statements of some other Christian bodies, the *Confession of Faith* for Cumberland Presbyerians is a relatively short volume. But that doesn't mean it is always easy to understand. Many people find it helpful to dig into the *Confession of Faith* in an intentional way in order to comprehend the insights of the church's doctrine.

Here are some tips for interpreting the *Confession of Faith*.

- Focus on the gospel of Jesus Christ as the main theme of the confession.

    The confession, like Scripture, points us to Jesus Christ.

- The Holy Spirit leads us to further and clearer understandings of Scripture and the *Confession of Faith*.

    The church has and will reinterpret or amend the *Confession of Faith* as the Holy Spirit leads.

- The *Confession of Faith* tries to tell the story the Bible tells.

    Every statement includes references from Scripure. Pay particular attention to the Scripture references for those statements you find confusing or difficult to understand.

- Studying the *Confession of Faith* is an important and helpful activity for all Cumberland Presbyterians.

    Consider gathering with others from your congregation to study the book together. Your pastor or church educator may be willing to lead a special study.

- Pay attention to the "flow" of the headings. This framework reveals something important about the way the church believes God is working in relationship to God's people.

    The headings are: God Speaks to the Human Family; The Human Family Breaks Relationship with God; God Acts through Jesus Christ to Reconcile the World; God Acts through the Holy Spirit; God Creates the Church for Mission; Christians Live and Witness in the World; God Consummates All Life and History.

TWO CREEDS

The two statements of faith that follow are ways by which Christians in different times and places have confessed their faith. The Apostles' and Nicene Creeds are from the period of the early church. They are used throughout the world as summaries of Christian faith. They unite Christians of all times and places with each other in the unity of faith (Ephesians 4:3, 13).

THE NICENE CREED

The Nicene Creed was the Christian church's first official statement of doctrine. It developed from the work of two ecumenical councils: Nicaea in A.D. 325 and Constantinople in A.D. 381. It was accepted as an authoritative statement by the Council of Chalcedon in A.D. 451. The Nicene Creed is the only creed accepted by all three major bodies of Christian churches: Eastern Orthodox, Roman Catholic, and Protestant. It affirms the Trinity, God is one God in three persons: Father, Son, and Holy Spirit, as well as the divinity and the humanity of Jesus Christ.

❶ The Nicene Creed (Ecumenical)

We believe in one God,
the Father, the Almighty,
maker of heaven and earth,
of all that is,
seen and unseen.

We believe in one Lord, Jesus Christ,
the only Son of God,
eternally begotten of the Father,
God from God, Light from Light,
true God from true God,
begotten, not made,
of one Being with the Father;
through him all things were made.
For us and for our salvation
he came down from heaven,
was incarnate of the Holy Spirit and the Virgin Mary
and became truly human.
For our sake he was crucified under Pontius Pilate;
he suffered death and was buried.

On the third day he rose again
in accordance with the Scriptures;
he ascended into heaven
and is seated at the right hand of the Father.
He will come again in glory to judge the living
and the dead,
and his kingdom will have no end.

We believe in the Holy Spirit, the Lord, the giver of life,
who proceeds from the Father and the Son,
who with the Father and the Son is worshiped
    and glorified,
who has spoken through the prophets.
We believe in one holy catholic and apostolic Church.
We acknowledge one baptism for the forgiveness of sins.
We look for the resurrection of the dead,
and the life of the world to come. Amen.

THE APOSTLES' CREED

The Apostles' Creed is the most widely used confession of faith in the Western church. It developed from the second to the ninth century. It was originally an early baptismal formula that grew to include the main, basic elements of Christian belief as "the rule of faith." It is now incorporated into the liturgies of many Sunday services of worship throughout the world. It affirms God as Father, Son, and Holy Spirit.

❶ The Apostles' Creed

I believe in God the Father Almighty, Maker of heaven and earth,

And in Jesus Christ his only Son our Lord; who was conceived by the Holy Ghost, born of the Virgin Mary, suffered under Pontius Pilate, was crucified, dead, and buried; he descended into hell; the third day he rose again from the dead; he ascended into heaven, and sitteth on the right hand of God the Father Almighty; from thence he shall come to judge the quick and the dead.

I believe in the Holy Ghost; the holy catholic Church; the communion of saints; the forgiveness of sins; the resurrection of the body; and the life everlasting. Amen.

CUMBERLAND PRESBYTERIAN CATECHISM

From New Testament times, one of the important ways Christians have taught doctrine is through the use of a catechism. A *catechism* is a summary of doctrine, often comprised of questions and answers about the teachings of faith. *Catechesis* was once a popular method of Christian education but began to be used less and less in Reformed churches in the twentieth century. In recent years, a number of Reformed churches have reclaimed catechesis as a unique and profitable method for teaching Christian faith to new generations of believers. Over the years, parents have often found the catechism to be a useful tool for teaching the faith to their children in the home.

The General Assembly of the Cumberland Presbyterian Church has adopted a catechetical study resource for use by local churches and groups interested in deepening their understanding of the *Confession of Faith*. This study resource includes eighty-three questions and answers that illuminate the main themes and beliefs of Cumberland Presbyterians. It is available online at www.cumberland.org on the General Assembly Office webpage.

CATECHETICAL RESOURCE: SELECTED Q&A

Who is God?

God is the one living, active Creator of all that is, seen and unseen.

Who are we?

We are a part of God's creation, made in God's own image. Our purpose is to love and serve God.

What is God like?

God is strong and wise.

God does what is good and right.

God speaks the truth.

God surrounds us always and everywhere.

God lives forever.

God never changes.

Above all, God is love.

How do we know God is love?

We know God is love because God gave the Son for us. Everyone who trusts the Son belongs to God's family, and will not perish, but will live with God now and forever.

How do we learn about God's love?

We learn about God's love from the Bible; through God's people, the church; in the events of naure and history;

and in many other ways; but most clearly through Jesus Christ.

What is the Bible?

The Bible is the Word of God, the written record of God's mighty acts.

What is grace?

Grace is the gift of God to all people. It is God's decision to create us, to care for us, and to claim us as children even though we do not deserve it. Grace cannot be earned. God gives all people the freedom to respond to God's grace.

What do we call our attempt to live without God?

Our attempt to live without God is called sin. Sin is disobedience to the revealed will of God.

Does God reject us when we sin?

No. God does not reject us when we sin. God loves us always.

How does God forgive us?

God starts over with us. God renews the relationship of grace with us, not counting our sins against us.

What do we call our relationship with God?

We call our relationship to God a covenant. God began the covenant long ago, has renewed it many times throughout the centuries, and has fulfilled it in the life, death, and resurrection of Jesus Christ. Still today, God upholds this covenant of grace.

Have people through the ages kept the covenant?

They have not, and neither do we.

Did God make Jesus suffer and die on the cross?

No. Jesus was willing to die for our sake.

What does the cross tell us about ourselves?

The cross tells us that our rebellion against God is serious.

What does the cross tell us about God?

The cross tells us that God's grace is greater than our sin. Human beings intended the cross for evil, but God used it for good.

What does it mean to be saved?

"To be saved" means to accept Jesus Christ as Lord and Savior, to live in the covenant of grace, and to promise, with the help of the Spirit, to follow God's will. Whoever is willing to be saved may be saved, but not without the help of the Spirit.

OPEN TO THE SPIRIT

Cumberland Presbyterians are proud of our doctrinal heritage. We believe our journey as a part of Christ's body in the world has made an important contribution to the evolution of Reformed theology in the last couple of centuries.

We trust that our doctrine is faithful to Scripture and to the witness of the Church through the years. We think our *Confession of Faith* is a reliable guide for those who want to follow the way of Jesus Christ.

The sometimes formal, often beautiful language of creeds, confessional statements, and catechisms can make them seem like the very "last word" in theology. But they are not. God alone is both the first and the final Word. As part of a community that is "Reformed and being reformed" we affirm that we want to be shaped by God—and not the other way around!

It is important for Christians always to be open as God the Holy Spirit offers us fresh insight and challenges us to greater faithfulness in loving God and one another

FOR FURTHER STUDY

This *Cumberland Presbyterian Handbook* has presented some basic descriptions of Cumberland Presbyterians. We come in many shapes and sizes, with many cultures, personalities, and desires.

A famous "bumper sticker" for one of the church's greatest theologians, Augustine, was "faith leads to understanding." When we have faith in Jesus Christ, we naturally and with great vigor want to learn more—about what God has done in Jesus Christ and what God is doing in the world today by the Holy Spirit.

Cumberland Presbyterians have always been Christians who have stressed learning, education, and growing in our Christian faith. Our faith is nurtured and made stronger as we come to know more about what we believe. We want our faith to lead us to further understanding.

The books here will help us grow in our understanding of Christian faith and our Cumberland Presbyterian tradition.

BOOKS FOR CUMBERLAND PRESBYTERIANS TO READ

Ben M. Barrus, Milton L. Baughn, & Thomas H. Campbell	*A People Called Cumberland Presbyterians*
Thomas D. Campbell	*One Family Under God*
Christopher Elwood	*Calvin for Armchair Theologians*
Ted V. Foote, Jr. and Alex Thornburg	*Being Presbyterian in the Bible Belt*
Matthew Gore	*A History of Cumberland Presbyterians in Kentucky*
Joe Ben Irby	*This They Believed*
James Knight	*Hearth and Chalice*
Donald K. McKim	*Presbyterian Beliefs: A Brief Introduction*
Hubert Morrow	*The Covenant of Grace: A Thread Through Scripture*
E.K. Reagin	*What Cumberland Presbyterians Believe*
James H. Smylie	*A Brief History of the Presbyterians*
Louis Weeks	*To Be a Presbyterian*
Louisa M. Woosley	*Shall Woman Preach? Or, The Question Answered*

For ordering information, contact:

Cumberland Presbyterian Resource Distribution
8207 Traditional Place
Cordova, TN 38016

901-276-4572, ext. 252
resources@cumberland.org

NOTES & STUFF

NOTES & STUFF

NOTES & STUFF

NOTES & STUFF

NOTES & STUFF

NOTES & STUFF

NOTES & STUFF

NOTES & STUFF

NOTES & STUFF

NOTES & STUFF

NOTES & STUFF

NOTES & STUFF

NOTES & STUFF

www.ingramcontent.com/pod-product-compliance
Lightning Source LLC
Chambersburg PA
CBHW051753040426
42446CB00007B/347